Reason at Work

philosophical papers

Reason at Work

philosophical papers

Jim Thornton

Diamond Harbour Press

Published by
Diamond Harbour Press
40 Ames Street
Paekakariki
New Zealand 5034
s.j.thornton18@gmail.com

First published January 2020

A catalogue record for this book is available from the
National Library of New Zealand

ISBN 978-0-473-47180-4

Book production and layout:
Rawhiti Editorial Services
rawhiti@snap.net.nz

Table of Contents

Foreword by Robert Stoothoff vii

Introduction xi

1. Can the Moral Point of View Be Justified? 1

2. Religious Belief and 'Reductionism' 19

3. Determinism and Moral Reactive Attitudes 46

4. The Alleged Limit to the Reach of Reason in Morality 72

5. Reason, Faith and Freedom 85

6. Human Rights 101

7. The Moral Responsibility of the Scientist 115

8. Miracles and God's Existence 122

9. The Morality of Nuclear Deterrence 139

10. Review of *Practical Medical Ethics* 159

11. Killing and Letting Die: a morally relevant distinction? 164

12. 'Killing, Letting Die and Moral Perception': a reply 169

13. A Sceptic's Tale 184

Foreword

In the morning of 27 September 2017, just short of his 89th birthday, Jim Thornton was giving a lecture on philosophy and the law at a U3A meeting, one of many such lectures he gave in the years of his retirement. As he began the lecture his vision became blurred and a headache developed to the extent that he could not continue. Soon after, he lapsed into unconsciousness, and he died a few days later at his home, surrounded by his family, having never regained consciousness. So ended Jim's love of philosophy that lasted the best part of six decades.

Jim began university studies in 1947 at Victoria University College (Wellington), and transferred to Canterbury University College (Christchurch) from which he graduated MA with first-class honours in philosophy. After theological studies at College House, Christchurch, and ordination in the Anglican Church, he joined the staff of the Anglican cathedral in Wellington, and served as vicar of Mangaweka before being appointed as a lecturer in Christian doctrine at the Anglican theological college based at College House. Subsequently Jim came to doubt the truth of major Christian doctrines and in 1967 he surrendered his licence as an 'officiating minister'. In the last essay of this collection, 'A Sceptic's Tale', he gives a clear and careful account of his abandonment of Christian beliefs. This essay, written in 2016, will provide readers with an excellent introduction to Jim's way of thinking.

Jim served as a temporary lecturer in philosophy at the University of Canterbury in 1956, joined the permanent staff in 1961, and retired in 1988 as a senior lecturer in the Department of Philosophy and Religious Studies. His main academic subjects were Moral Philosophy and the Philosophy of Religion. He was an exemplary colleague. In fact, during the 1970s and 1980s all the members of the Department of Philosophy and Religious Studies at the University of Canterbury were exemplary colleagues – so much so that we had almost no need for departmental meetings, which pleased all of us (and, I suspect, especially Jim).

Despite his distaste for meetings, Jim gave significant service as a member of university governing bodies and committees. Perhaps the most significant committee on which he served was that established in 1977 to select a new Vice-Chancellor. This committee was significant because its deliberations resulted in the appointment of Bert Brownlie, which ushered in a period that made Canterbury (quoting from the 1988 *Chronicle* article reporting Jim's retirement): "the happiest of universities and probably the envy of all other New Zealand universities".

In 2016 Jim collected twelve of his publications in a booklet which he described as "a selection from those of my writings on philosophy which I still think are of some merit and which I hope may be of interest to those members of my family who have a philosophical bent (or warp?)".

In my opinion, shared by Jim's ex-colleagues, these papers have such great merit that they deserve to be made available for a wider audience than the members of his family. Hence this volume, which reproduces the papers collected in that booklet.

Jim's approach to philosophical problems was, broadly speaking, analytic. He saw the task of philosophy as that of seeking to resolve, if not solve, problems by clarifying the underlying concepts so as to allow rational discussion of the central issues – that is, discussion which is unimpeded by the confusions, prejudices, preconceptions, pretensions, ungrounded intuitions, intellectual and emotional baggage, &c that are apt to encumber our thinking about these issues. Such discussion may not serve to solve or resolve the problems, and indeed may result in the conclusion that they are pseudo-problems. But even this conclusion would constitute philosophical progress in so far as the analyses and arguments that lead to it enhance our understanding of the issues.

Jim applied this approach both to traditional problems of philosophy, such as free will and determinism, the existence of God, and the nature of moral judgements, and – especially in his later years – to substantive moral issues, such as euthanasia, human rights, and the morality of nuclear deterrence.

Jim wrote an important paper on the morality of nuclear deterrence in 1986. In it he argues with great force that acceptance of a nuclear deterrence policy has no moral justification. Here is the conclusion:

> …to accept the nuclear deterrence policy…is to endorse a policy which necessarily involves being ready now, should circumstances demand it, to unleash forces whose evil effects would be literally mind-boggling and which would, it is freely admitted, be unredeemed by any consequential good. To be thoroughly prepared to do this, however unlikely we think it might be necessary, is surely already to have abandoned every moral ideal of freedom, justice, compassion and goodness to which civilized human beings have aspired. But to be thoroughly prepared to do this precisely in order to preserve and defend those ideals can be nothing less than the ultimate in moral absurdity.

The reasoning by which he reaches this conclusion is a model of philosophical analysis.

Medical ethics was one of Jim's main interests in his retirement, and he wrote wrote several papers on the subject of euthanasia. Of special importance is his submission in January 2016 to the parliamentary select committee considering proposed legislation on euthanasia. Here again, I can do no better than quote Jim's words:

> I have outlined a prima facie case for the view that in a carefully qualified context of medical care there is no ethically relevant difference between, on the one hand, actively killing a patient in response to their rational and measured request, and on the other of allowing a patient to die from the effects of the withdrawal of life-preserving treatment in response to their similarly qualified request. If the latter is not merely justifiable, but indeed both morally and legally obligatory, then so is the former. Whether this argument is convincing or not is a matter of controversy among professional ethicists. What is beyond question is its central importance to any informed, rational discussion of euthanasia and the related topic of assisted suicide. If the argument is flawed it needs to be shown to be so.

Jim notes that the issue he raises here is centrally important to the euthanasia debate, but has largely been neglected both by politicians and by the general public. He would have been pleased to see discussion of this crucial point emerging in recent debates.

In preparing Jim's papers for publication, I have made some minor editorial changes for the sake of consistency in spelling and punctuation, and a few more substantial changes, of which I'm sure Jim would have approved. For their help in preparing this volume I wish to thank Jim's wife, daughter and eldest son – Ann, Rachel and Stephen; Jim's ex-colleagues, Jim Wilson and Colin Brown; his student Sylvia Borren; and John Burt.

Robert Stoothoff

Introduction

The following papers are a selection from those of my writings on philosophy which I still think are of some merit and which I hope may be of interest to those members of my family who have a philosophical bent (or warp?). Some of the papers belong to that branch of philosophy known as the philosophy of religion but they have, I believe, a philosophical relevance quite independent of any interest one may have in religion.

On reflection, my life-long interest in philosophy has been focused mainly on those aspects of religious and moral claims made by theologians and philosophers which, if true, are of considerable importance for our understanding of what it means to be human. Unfortunately, such claims have too often tended to suffer from an exasperating obscurity with respect to both their meaning and foundation. In short, most of my papers are what in the trade are sometimes called "hatchet jobs". To what extent I have succeeded in my modest attempts to dispel this obscurity and thereby discover what truth, if any, lies within them is of course for others to judge.

At the end of each of most of the papers I have added a postscript. In many cases, reading the postscript before reading the paper itself may help to make it more intelligible. The postscript added to the paper 'The Morality of Nuclear Deterrence' is longer than the others as it seemed helpful in this case to give some account of its provenance. I regard that essay as perhaps the most carefully argued of all my philosophical writings, as its subject-matter is certainly the most important.

Jim Thornton
August 2016

1

Can the Moral Point of View be Justified?[1]

In his Introduction to *The Moral Point of View*[2] Professor Baier mentions what he regards as "three fundamental questions of ethics requiring unequivocal and reassuring answers". The first of these questions, which he clearly regards as the most important, is this: "Should anyone do what is right when doing so is not to his advantage and if so why?"[3] Concerning this question he says, "If we could prove that we really should do what is right and refrain from doing what is wrong by pointing to a good reason why we should, we could remove the most serious of all our doubts (that is, as far as doubts about ethics are concerned), the doubt whether morality is indeed a sensible 'game', a practice worth preserving and worth conforming to".[4] It is this question, and two of the attempts made to answer it, including Baier's own, that I want to discuss in this article. I shall therefore be concerned with the more difficult task of giving a correct analysis of what "the moral point of view" is only in so far as it is necessary to do this in order to discuss the problem of its 'justification'.

This approach might at once be criticised as putting the cart before the horse. Surely, it will be objected, nothing fruitful can be said about the justification of the moral point of view unless it is preceded by a full discussion as to what is *meant* by this expression. (Plato I think would go further and say that *only* by seeing clearly what the moral point of view is can we understand how its adoption is justified, and in a way this is what I want to argue myself.) Yet sometimes an examination of the cart can tell us quite a lot about the sort of animal that pulls it. What is logically a prior question is not always methodological-wise the best question to tackle first.

Furthermore, there is something queer about the question "Why should I adopt the moral point of view?" which is missing in the relatively straightforward but nevertheless more difficult question "What constitutes the moral point of view?" and this queerness gives the former question a certain urgency.

But not everyone would agree that Baier's fundamental question is queer. Or, if it is admitted to be queer, it is sometimes thought to be none the less important for being that, and one which still needs answering. On the other hand, others have suspected that its queerness is directly related to its being a pseudo-question, a question which cannot be answered because nothing could logically count as an answer to it; and if we discover that a question is logically impossible to answer this is the same thing as saying that what we were trying to answer could not have been a genuine question after all. That Baier's 'fundamental' question is indeed a pseudo-question is, I think, a view widely held nowadays, and it is also with some qualifications my own view. Nevertheless, Baier's book has attracted a good deal of attention and admiration, not the least of which is directed to the way he has taken seriously this so-called pseudo-question. Furthermore, it seems to me that no one (except perhaps Professor D. H. Monro) has expressed quite so forcibly as Baier has the usual arguments for regarding it as a pseudo-question. Yet both Baier and Monro regard these arguments as less than conclusive. Baier obviously thinks that he has provided a satisfactory answer to this "fundamental question of ethics", and of course if he has provided a satisfactory answer to it then the arguments pointing to its being a pseudo-question must all be fallacious. (Pseudo-questions presumably can have pseudo-answers, but not satisfactory answers, or for that matter, unsatisfactory answers.) In his Critical Notice of

Baier's book Monro argues convincingly that Baier has *not* provided a satisfactory answer to the question, but at the same time he commends Baier for taking it seriously.[5] Monro sees this question as one which was raised and given one sort of answer by Hobbes, and he thinks that if we are not prepared to accept Hobbes's own answer (or Baier's for that matter) we are nevertheless still left with Hobbes's question. "It is time," he says, "that someone realised that Hobbesism deserves a more convincing answer than it has yet been given".[6]

The question, of course, is older than Hobbes. Baier's formulation of it, "Should anyone do what is right when doing so is not to his advantage and if so why?", is perhaps not a bad paraphrase of the question which Thrasymachus raised, and which Glaucon and Adeimantus forcibly put to Socrates, in the first two books of Plato's *Republic*. It is often shortened to something like "Why should I be moral?" or "Why should I be just?" or "What is the ultimate justification of morals?" These are all variations on the one theme and all of them, I believe, are equally suspicious. I propose therefore to examine some recent attempts to persuade us that our suspicions are unfounded and that these are genuine questions which deserve to be taken seriously

I have already mentioned that Baier himself is quite well aware that there are arguments which provide a prima facie case against the genuineness of his "fundamental question of ethics" (though in his view they provide only a prima facie case). The substance of one such argument is as follows:[7]

> Whenever we are offered reasons why we should adopt a proposed course of action, or why we should do A rather than B, then either it makes sense to ask why we should accept these as good or sufficient reasons or else it does not make sense. In cases where it does make sense to ask why the reasons should be accepted, it will be because more ultimate reasons can be given. If and when these

> more ultimate reasons are given, again either it will make sense to ask why these should be accepted or it will not make sense to ask this. Where it does make sense, the same question can be repeated, and so on. Now this process of pushing back to more and more basic reasons for practical choice cannot go on ad infinitum. There must always come a point when it just does not make sense to ask, "Why should I accept this as a reason for doing A, or avoiding B, etc.?" When this point has been reached, one has been given an 'ultimate reason' why a proposed course of action should be pursued or avoided, and, by definition, one cannot ask for a reason for accepting what is itself an ultimate reason.

Now obviously everything depends, in this argument, on whether we can agree on what sort of reason will count as an 'ultimate reason'. One plausible candidate for this is 'self-interest'. That self-interest is an ultimate reason in this sense is generally thought to be illustrated by this well-known passage from Hume:

> Ask a man why he uses exercise; he will answer, because he desires to keep his health. If you then enquire why he desires health, he will readily reply, because sickness is painful. If you push your enquiries farther, and desire a reason why he hates pain, it is impossible he can give any. This is an ultimate end, and is never referred to any other object.[8]

It is an ultimate end because, generally speaking, the avoidance of pain is agreed to be in one's best interests, and so, unless there are complicating circumstances, no better reason can be given for doing something than to show that it is in one's best interests to do it.

But, of course, there sometimes are complicating circumstances, e.g. when a moral issue is at stake. So it seems that a rival candidate for the position of an ultimate reason is the 'moral reason'. If A says to B, "Why should I keep my promise to marry Jane?" then on the one hand A might be asking B for a justification of the general practice of promise-keeping ("What is the point of keeping promises anyway?"). On the other hand, A might be thinking of his own particular situation and asking B to show him why he should keep his particular promise to Jane, hinting that perhaps his situation should be regarded as exceptional because of special extenuating circumstances. On either of these interpretations his question would be perfectly proper. But if, in the course of further discussion, A says, "Oh I know that it would be morally wrong for me to break my promise to marry Jane, but why should I keep my promise?" then would not this be a very odd remark to make? Surely once a moral reason for a proposed course of action has been given and accepted as relevant, no further justification for doing the action is called for. What could be a better reason for doing something than a moral reason?

Thus (the argument runs) we have two kinds of ultimate reasons for action – moral reasons and reasons of self-interest. Moreover, nothing else will be found to function as an ultimate reason apart from these two. Only reasons of self-interest and moral reasons can put a logical stop to a series of questions of the form "Why should I do X?"

Now the really serious complication arises when these two sorts of ultimate reason conflict, i.e. when we have a proposed course of action such that, on the grounds of our best interests, we should do it, but on moral grounds we should refrain from doing it. In such cases the reason which is said to have the greater weight is the moral reason, i.e. we should do what is right even when it is not to our advantage to do so. But it will not make sense to ask "Why?". To ask for a reason for a proposed course of action is to ask to be shown either that the action will be conducive to one's best interests or else that it is demanded by one's moral code. Now in the case in point the action is by definition not in one's best interests, so this prevents 'self-interest' from functioning as an ultimate reason. But we are asking why we should do what our moral code demands for us, so we can't be given a moral reason why we should be moral. But there aren't any other kinds of ultimate reasons apart from moral reasons and reasons of self-interest. Therefore, the question "Why should I do what is right when it is not in my interests to do so?" is logically impossible to answer and is merely a pseudo-question.

So much for the prima facie case for the logical absurdity of Baier's fundamental question of ethics. How strong an argument is it? Its weakest point would seem to be the apparently arbitrary and dogmatic assertion that in situations where moral duty and self-interest conflict it is the moral reason which has the greater weight. There seems to be some sort of logical slide between how much weight a reason has and how much weight a reason is to be given. What is it to say that moral reasons are weightier than reasons of self-interest if it is not to say that moral reasons should be given greater weight than reasons of self-interest? If this is what is meant, it seems intolerable that this claim cannot be justified rationally. It is all very well to mention that we have been taught from childhood to regard the moral reasons as being weightier. This merely makes us demand all the more urgently that we be shown that what we have been taught in childhood has some rational basis, and it is just this that Baier felt called upon to provide. He thinks he can show that there are weightier reasons, that it is more rational, to do what is right than to do what is simply in our own interests. But he argues that if someone were then to ask "Why should we be rational?" then this would be a nonsensical question because following reason is just doing what is supported by the weightiest reasons, and it does not make sense to ask for reasons for doing what is supported by the weightiest reasons.[9]

This looks like a promising move, but, of course, the crucial question is: Does Baier succeed in showing that there are weightier reasons for doing what is right than for following our own interests? In one sense he does, but unfortunately not in the sense required by his original "fundamental" question. All he succeeds in showing is Hobbes's point, viz. that there are weightier reasons for everyone doing what is right than for everyone following self-interest.[10] Baier asks us to examine "the two alternative worlds, one in which moral reasons are always treated by everyone as superior to reasons of self-interest and one in which the reverse is the practice. And we can see that the first world is the better world, because we can see that the second world would be the sort which Hobbes describes as "the state of nature"[11]. Baier concludes that the answer to the question "Why should we be moral?" is as follows:

> We should be moral because being moral is following rules designed to overrule self-interest whenever it is in the interest of everyone alike that everyone should set aside his interest. . . . It is not possible that everyone should do better for himself by following enlightened self-interest rather than morality. The best possible life for everyone is attainable only by everyone's following the rules of morality, that is, rules which quite frequently may require individuals to make genuine sacrifices.[12]

It is clear, I think, that Baier has not answered his original question. His mistake was to think that what we have to do to answer it is to consider two alternative worlds, the one in which moral rules are universally followed and the one in which the rules of enlightened self-interest are universally followed, and then decide which is the better world to live in, i.e. in our own better interests. But if we are going to answer along these lines his fundamental question of ethics, viz. "Why should I be moral when doing so is not to my advantage?", then there are not just two alternative worlds which we have to compare but three. The third possible world is the one in which moral rules are obeyed by everyone else except me, who follows enlightened self-interest. The first world is admittedly, from everyone's point of view, a better alternative to the second, but is not the third world, from my point of view, a better alternative to either of the other two? Of course, one can hold that the third world is not a practical possibility, but Baier has made it plain that he does not support this view. He makes it quite clear that following morality entails making "genuine sacrifices" and he is not convinced by those who would argue that following morality is in the long run identical with following enlightened self-interest. Inevitably, then, his attempt to give the moral point of view a rational basis comes to grief because, in spite of what he says to the contrary, he has assumed that the only really ultimate reason justifying an action is in fact self-interest, and so he is logically prevented from justifying doing one's moral duty in those situations in which duty and interest really do conflict.

My guess is that he was probably prevented from seeing the glaring self-contradiction in his argument by a simple verbal confusion. It is significant that in the early stages of his book he frequently expresses his "fundamental question of ethics" in the words "Why should *I* be moral?" (my italics). However, at the end of the book, when he is at last ready to try to answer the question, he invariably expresses it in the words "Why should we be moral?" This latter question can easily be interpreted as a demand for a rational justification of the institution of morality in general, and, of course, a plausible answer can be given to this question along more or less Hobbesian lines. But to answer this general question is not automatically to have answered the particular and very different question, "Why should I be moral (in the particular situation x at time t) ?", and yet Baier has tended to use these two ways of expressing his guestion indifferently as if they meant the same thing.

My conclusion at this point is that Baier has not succeeded in answering his “fundamental question of ethics” and therefore has not succeeded in showing that it is a genuine question demanding a serious answer. But, of course, it may still be true that the question is in fact a genuine one.

Another philosopher who has taken the question seriously and whose articles on moral philosophy have caused much favourable comment is Mrs Philippa Foot. In an article called ‘Moral Beliefs’[13] she considers the question ‘Why should I be just?’. This question, it is true, is not verbally identical with Baier’s, but I think the context of her discussion shows that in substance the point at issue is the same. The main purpose of her article, however, is to show that the case for “ethical naturalism” is much stronger than is generally admitted. She argues that not any sort of belief can function as a moral belief which is not necessarily related in some way to human welfare, and that what constitutes human welfare is very far from being a wholly arbitrary matter of opinion. For example, she argues that it would be as plausible for someone to hold that prudence, courage or temperance were not virtues as it would be to hold that the loss of one’s hands or eyes were not injuries. With this part of her argument I am not immediately concerned and have no particular quarrel.

But the virtue of ‘justice’ raises a different problem for, as she says, “While prudence, courage and temperance are qualities which benefit the man who has them, justice seems rather to benefit others, and to work to the disadvantage of the just man himself . . . We will be asked,” she continues, “how on our theory justice can be a virtue and injustice a vice, since it will surely be difficult to show that any man whatsoever must need to be just as he needs the use of his hands and eyes, or needs prudence, courage and temperance?”[14] Mrs Foot believes that Thrasymachus's argument has to be taken with complete seriousness and that if his premiss is true, viz. that injustice is more profitable than justice, then his conclusion certainly follows, viz. that a man who has the strength to get away with injustice has reason to follow this as the best way of life. "It is a striking fact about modern moral philosophy," she says, "that no one sees any difficulty in accepting Thrasymachus's premiss and rejecting his conclusion."[15]

It is only fair to point out that at least Baier saw this to be a difficulty but, as we have seen, he rejected Thrasymachus's conclusion without being successful in rejecting his premiss. I now want to try to show that Mrs Foot has not fared any better. In fact I believe she is guilty of much the same kind of confusion· as Baier. Nevertheless, in her article she makes a number of valuable points relevant to what I believe is the correct conclusion to be drawn, but which in fact tend to strengthen the case against her.

Like Baier, she stresses the difficulty of showing that it is always profitable for the good man to be just or moral, and yet at the same time she is convinced that, unless this is done, no reason has been given why the good man should be just.

> Given Thrasymachus's premiss, Thrasymachus's point of view is reasonable; we have no particular reason to admire those who practise justice through timidity or stupidity.[16]

But she tries to have it both ways. From having insisted on the reality of the situation in which justice and self-interest are incompatible, she moves on to make a strong suggestion that the conflict in these situations is more apparent than real and that in most if not all cases it will be found that it really is profitable for the good man to be just after all:

> Is it true, however, to say that justice is not something a man needs in his dealings with his fellows, supposing

> only that he be strong? Those who think that he can get on perfectly well without being just should be asked to say exactly how such a man is supposed to live. We know that he is to practise injustice whenever the unjust act would bring him advantage; but what is he to say? Does he admit that he does not recognise the rights of other people, or does he pretend? In the first case even those who combine with him will know that on a change of fortune, or a shift of affection, he may turn to plunder them, and he must be as wary of their treachery as they are of his. Presumably the happy unjust man is supposed, as in Book II of the *Republic,* to be a very cunning liar and actor, combining complete injustice with the appearance of justice: he is prepared to treat others ruthlessly, but pretends that nothing is further from his mind. Philosophers often speak as if a man could thus hide himself even from those around him, but the supposition is doubtful, and in any case the price in vigilance would be colossal.[17]

Then finally (and here the pendulum swings back once more) Mrs Foot admits that of course there will be some situations in which justice is not profitable, but, because a man has a reason to be just on most occasions, he cannot act differently in these highly exceptional circumstances without forfeiting his right to be called a just man. Here I quote her final paragraph:

> The reason why it seems to some people so impossibly difficult to show that justice is more profitable than injustice is that they consider in isolation particular just acts. It is perfectly true that if a man is just it follows that he will be prepared, in the event of very evil circumstances, even to face death rather than to act unjustly – for instance, in getting an innocent man convicted of a crime of which he has been accused. For him it turns out that his justice brings disaster on him,

> and yet like anyone else he had good reason to be a just and not an unjust man. He could not have it both ways and while possessing the virtue of justice hold himself ready to be unjust should any great advantage accrue. The man who has the virtue of justice is not ready to do certain things, and if he is too easily tempted we shall say that he was ready after all.

But surely this last point is strictly irrelevant, for it is not disputed that the man who acts unjustly when it suits his long-term interest is anything but unjust. Of course he is unjust and immoral – but is he irrational? And the man who does not yield to temptation is quite rightly called a just man. But is he rightly called a rational man? These are the doubts which Thrasymachus raised and these are the doubts which Mrs Foot set out to remove, but it is quite plain that she has not removed them. Or rather, by the way in which she interprets the term "rational" she ensures that the doubts are removed (as it were) in the other direction, for on her own premisses it indeed follows inevitably that a man has no reason to be consistently just, for on some occasions he will see that to act justly will bring disaster upon him.

There is, it is true, an alternative conclusion which can be drawn from her argument, viz. that if nothing is to be allowed to count as a virtue unless it is invariably profitable to its possessor, then justice is not a virtue. But it is clear that this conclusion does not suit her purpose either, because, as she denies the consequent (she is sure that justice *is* a virtue), she is logically committed to denying the antecedent, which asserts that being profitable to its possessor is part of what is *meant* by the term virtue. Yet it was precisely in order to *affirm* this antecedent or something very like it, that she wrote the article I have been discussing.

We are now in a position to ask whether the failure of both Baier and Mrs Foot to answer the question "Why should

I be moral (or just) when it is not to my advantage?" is not after all related to its being a pseudo-question, and clearly it is so related. Despite explicit claims to the contrary on Baier's part, both he and Mrs Foot have in fact treated self-interest as the only really ultimate justifying reason for action. This being so, it follows that it is logically impossible for them to justify any action whatever, moral or otherwise, which is not in the agent's supposed long-term self-interest. Once it is admitted that there are situations in which duty and self-interest genuinely conflict, then it follows that either following duty in such cases is irrational or self-interest is not the only ultimate justifying reason. Furthermore, it seems likely that both Baier and Mrs Foot were prevented from seeing that they were attempting the logically impossible principally because they both repeatedly confuse the task of justifying particular moral acts with the very different task of justifying the general institution of morality.

However, though the question which Baier and Mrs Foot set themselves to answer was, given their particular assumptions, logically unanswerable, it seems it would still have been a pseudo-question even had they assumed that moral reasons are also to be counted as genuinely 'ultimate reasons'. Just what sort of reason could we have in the context of a particular situation for choosing to follow morality rather than enlightened self-interest?

Someone who sees the force of this argument might be tempted to say, "Of course no rational justification can be given for accepting the moral point of view, because to say 'I should do what is right even when it is not to my ultimate advantage' is to express a kind of leap of faith". In fact, however, all that it expresses is either a tautology or a contradiction. If "should" is being used here in its moral sense (as it often is) then it is tautologous to say that we should be moral even when it is not to our advantage, for this is part of what "being moral" means.

But if "should" is being used in its self-interest sense (as again it often is) then it is just plain self-contradictory to say that we should be moral even when it is not to our advantage. And it is hard to see what other sense, apart from these two, the word 'should' could have in the context of this expression. (This point, by the way, was first brought home to me by Professor Shorter.)

Yet, in spite of all that has been said, it still remains true, of course, that the point of view of enlightened self-interest is different from the moral point of view – not merely theoretically different but also different in practice. It seems that it is possible to accept the moral point of view or to reject it, and, according to the choice one makes, there will be some situations in which different courses of action will be followed. The rational egoist[18] will follow the rules of morality only to the extent that doing so will further his long-term interests, and to this extent, of course, the conduct of the rational egoist will be identical with the conduct of the morally good man. But in those Gyges-like situations where there is a genuine conflict between moral duty and long-term self-interest, the rational egoist (provided he does not on these occasions act irrationally) will do one thing and the morally good man (provided he does not on these occasions act immorally) will do another. Yet, as we have seen, neither the point of view of rational egoism nor the point of view of morality can be justified rationally without begging questions concerning the meaning of the word "rational".

But, it may now be objected, is there not an asymmetry about the contrast which demands some sort of explanation? For in the Gyges-like situation, if the egoist does not do what is in his own interests we say he acted irrationally, whereas if in the same situation the morally good man does not do his duty we say he acted immorally but we do not say he acted irrationally. This suggests that it is only the point of view of rational egoism which is truly rational, and that self-interest is the only genuinely 'ultimate reason' after all.

But let us look again at the reasons why self-interest is thought to put an effective logical stop to the question-series "Why should I do X?" In her article, Mrs Foot correctly observes that "in general anyone is given a reason for acting when he is shown the way to something he wants".[19] If someone wants X, and we show that the way to X is to do Y, we have given him a reason for doing Y. But have we given him an ultimate reason? Only, I think, if we have shown him the way to that which, of all the practical possibilities open to him, he wants most of all in the particular circumstances in which he finds himself. But it may be that what he wants most of all is to do his moral duty. Then if X is his moral duty, we have given him an ultimate reason for doing Y once we have shown him that Y is the particular act which in the circumstances moral duty requires him to do.

Thus it is what we most want to do, rather than what is in our own self-interest that provides the basis for the ultimate rational justification for action. Moreover, it just seems to be a brute fact about human nature that we do not all agree as to what we most want to do even when the 'wants' are of a highly general sort. Whereas some people want most of all to do whatever is in their own best interests, there are others, it seems, who, at least from time to time, most want to do whatever is their moral duty, even if this is at the cost of their own best interests.

The fact that not all of us want to do our moral duty, and even if most of us do, we do not always want to, or we do not always want to do it most of all, has misled some philosophers into thinking that if anything is going to function as an ultimate reason it will have to be something which everyone always wants most of all. They have seen that unless this is so we can never be sure that we have given a person an ultimate reason for doing an action, for if what we gave as a reason was not something that pointed the way to what that person wanted most of all at that particular time, it would always be sensible for him to reply "But why should I do X?". This is the point Mrs Foot is making in the following passage:

> In general, anyone is given a reason for acting when he is shown the way to something he wants; but for some wants the question "Why do you want that?" will make sense, and for others it will not . . . This is why it is not true to say that "It's unjust" gives a reason in so far as any reasons can ever be given. "It's unjust" gives a reason only if the nature of justice can be shown to be such that it is necessarily connected with what a man wants.[20]

The correct conclusion to draw, however, is not that the avoidance of a particular unjust action will be rationally justified only if we connect it with something that everyone always wants, but rather only if it is connected with what is wanted most of all by the particular person concerned at that particular time. For there seems to be no highly general 'want' which all of us always want fulfilled more than anything else, and in particular it is not true that what all of us at all times most want is whatever is in our own long-term best interests.

My general conclusions are as follows:

(1) That the so-called fundamental question of ethics which both Baier and Mrs Foot have attempted to answer has not been answered by either of them because, basically, it is a pseudo-question after all.

(2) That in situations where there is a genuine conflict between moral duty and enlightened self-interest, whichever course of action is followed will either be rational or irrational according to whether or not the agent accepts or rejects the moral point of view,

(3) That it is what a person most wants to do, rather than what is in his own best interests, that provides the ultimate basis for the rational justification of an action.

Notes

1. This article, published in *The Australasian Journal of Philosophy* 42 (1964), is a slightly revised version of a paper read at the NZ Philosophy Conference at Wellington in May 1963.
2. Kurt Baier, *The Moral Point of View* (Cornell University Press, 1958).
3. *The Moral Point of View*, p. 3.
4. *The Moral Point of View*, p. 4.
5. See *The Australasian Journal of Philosophy*, May, 1959.
6. *Ibid.*, p. 78.
7. Here I am freely drawing upon and expressing in my own way many of the points that Baier makes in Ch. 1, Section 1, and elsewhere in his book.
8. *Enquiries*, Appendix I, v.
9. *The Moral Point of View*, p. 318.
10. See D. H. Munro's 'Critical Notice', *loc cit.* pp. 77f.
11. *The Moral Point of View*, p. 310.
12. *The Moral Point of View*, pp. 314f.
13. *Proceedings of the Aristotelian Society*, Supplementary Volume 1958–59.
14. 'Moral Beliefs', p. 99.
15. 'Moral Beliefs', p. 100.
16. 'Moral Beliefs', p. 102.
17. 'Moral Beliefs', p. 103.
18. For the purposes of this article it will be sufficient to define "rational egoist" as one who accept as his own basic guide to action the principle of enlightened self-interest.

19. 'Moral Beliefs', p. 101.
20. 'Moral Beliefs', p. 101.

Postscript

This was my first article to be published. A few years after it had appeared in The Australasian Journal of Philosophy it was reprinted in Readings in Contemporary Ethical Theory, edited by Kenneth Pahel and Marvin Schiller (Prentice-Hall, 1970). Those who had given it favourable comment included William Frankena (Michigan University) and Kai Nielsen (New York University) who also contributed to the above-mentioned Readings on the same topic. (Kai told me that if he had read my article before writing his, his would have been very different).

One justified criticism of my essay made by more than one critic is that it was 'unfinished'. Certainly a lot more needed to be said about the complex concept of 'wants' and how that concept is connected with reasons for action and the general notion of rationality. I attempted to remedy this weakness in the paper 'The alleged limit of the reach of reason in morality' (Ch. 4 below), which is part of a paper titled 'Wants, Beliefs and Reasons for Action,' which I read at the NZ Philosophy Conference at Waikato University in 1973.

2

Religious Belief and 'Reductionism':

when is an analysis of religious belief a 'reductionist' analysis?

It has frequently been claimed that a great deal of contemporary philosophy of religion is 'reductionist' in that, instead of giving a philosophical account of the nature of religious belief, philosophers have produced an analysis of something which is very much less; and if they have tried to give an account of the nature of specifically Christian belief they have characteristically served up extremely eviscerated versions of Christianity, the complaint has run.

I want to examine this contention, for although, on the face of it, nothing seems to be more certain than that it is not merely possible, but likely, that whoever embarks upon a philosophical analysis of the nature of religious belief will do less than full justice to that extremely complex phenomenon, it can hardly be just this almost inevitable falling short of the ideal that is being complained of, or else we should have to regard all philosophies of religion as more or less 'reductionist'. On the other hand, if we reserve this term for the more conspicuous failures, then not only shall we need to make clear the criteria by which we are measuring the degree of relative success, but also we shall need to avoid giving the impression that the cutting line between pass and failure is a purely arbitrary one. What I want to show is not that the distinction between 'reductionist' and 'non-reductionist' analyses of religious belief is necessarily a spurious one, but that the provision of satisfactory criteria on the basis of which the distinction may justifiably be drawn is considerably less straightforward than some of the philosophers who have been vocal on the subject seem to have assumed.

Just as complaints against reductionism have come from a wide range of philosophical points of view, so also those who have been the objects of attack are representative of traditions equally varied. For example, the objectors include C. B. Martin, E. L. Mascall and Ninian Smart, who could no more be described as belonging to a common 'school of thought' than could those whom they have attacked, such as R. B. Braithwaite, Paul Tillich and Schubert Ogden.

Faced, therefore, with such a variety of plaintiffs and defendants it will not be my purpose to try to give a comprehensive survey of all those philosophies of religion which have been denounced as reductionist, nor will I be concerned to search for some allegedly common factor shared by them or their critics. Where both philosophical and religious ancestry is so mixed and uncertain, even to look for familiar resemblances seems optimistic. Instead, what I propose to do is to examine one or two examples of recent complaints against reductionism and, on this basis, risk a few cautious generalisations.

Orthodox/traditionalist attacks on 'reductionism'

I want to turn first to E. L. Mascall's recent book *The Secularisation of Christianity*[1], which is perhaps the most vigorous as it is certainly the most erudite attack on so-called 'reductionist' versions of Christianity that has so far appeared. His principal targets are Paul van Buren's *The Secular Meaning of the Gospel* and John Robinson's notorious *Honest to God*, though a number of other writers who also come under heavy fire include R. B. Braithwaite[2], T. R. Miles, Paul Tillich, Dietrich Bonhoeffer, Rudolph Bultmann and S. M. Ogden. Now all these writers could be said to have attempted, each in his own way, to express Christian belief in terms which are 'relevant' and 'meaningful' to the contemporary age. Such attempts Mascall regards as, in themselves, perfectly legitimate, even laudable and necessary, provided only that in seeking to re-express the traditional doctrines the doctrines themselves are not changed or emasculated. But this, he claims, is precisely what happened to them at the hands of these writers. At the beginning of chapter one of his book (significantly entitled 'The Changeless and the Changing') he quotes with approval some words of Pope John XXIII :

> The substance of the ancient doctrine, contained in the 'deposit of faith' is one thing; its formulation is quite another.

Mascall then goes on to observe,

> One of the most imperative duties with which the Christian theologian is confronted is that of relating the revealed datum of Christian truth, final, absolute, and fundamentally permanent as he must by his Christian commitment believe it to be, to the essentially incomplete, relative and constantly changing intellectual framework of the world in which he lives. This is a task of great importance and of no less difficulty, and it is, I venture to suggest, highly unfortunate that many of those writers who have recently addressed themselves to it because they were convinced of its importance have assumed it to be very much easier than in fact it is.[3]

I am not sure whether the difficulty which Mascall has in mind here is essentially that of finding ways of giving contemporary expression to Christian beliefs, or that of the related but logically prior difficulty of distinguishing what Pope John called 'the substance of the ancient doctrine' from its formulations, whether ancient or modern. Indeed, elsewhere in the chapter he shows that he is aware of both difficulties, but it is the latter which receives the scanter treatment, and yet it is surely the one which deserves the closer examination. For unless it is possible, at least in principle, to distinguish the 'substance' of the doctrine from the way in which it is formulated, the question as to whether or not modern so-called secularised interpretations of Christianity have resulted in throwing out the baby with the bathwater will not even arise. Mascall's relatively superficial treatment of this question is all the more surprising in view of the fact that the main argument of his book is to prove that secularist interpreters of Christianity like van Buren and Bishop Robinson have in fact abandoned baby, bathwater and all.[4] It could be said against Mascall (adopting his own words) that if it is an imperative duty of the Christian theologian to distinguish the unchanging substance of the ancient doctrine from its temporary and variable formulations, one writer who has deplored the modern neglect of this duty has assumed its performance to be very much easier than in fact it is.

That the difficulties of distinguishing the so-called 'substance' of the doctrine from its variable linguistic formulations are indeed formidable is in part brought out by Mascall's patently inadequate suggestions as to how such a distinction might be made. He clearly recognises that the 'substance' cannot be specified by "laying down some unalterable form of words, for this would be simply an additional formulation";[5] and he explicitly rejects that point of view (examples of which he finds in both Protestant and Catholic traditions) which "would deem some particular verbal formula or body of verbal formulas as expressing the Gospel exhaustively, finally and with complete adequacy forChristians of every epoch, locality, race, culture, and individual mental equipment."[6] But when Mascall makes his own suggestions as to how the substance of the Gospel is to be recognised and specified he is much less satisfactory, and at the very point of his argument on which is pivoted his whole case against the reductionists – the point, that is, at which he needs to be the most clear – he lapses into theological jargon of the most opaque variety. Here I shall need to quote him at length:

> How then, is the theologian to maintain his loyalty to the revealed Gospel, while at the same time making every effort to express it in terms intelligible to its hearers and to help them to see its implication for their particular circumstances and situations? It is, I suggest, by forming a deliberate habit of loyal submission to Christian tradition, while at the same time bringing to bear upon it all the critical and interpretative gifts which God has given him . . .While all formulations of Christian truth, even the most authoritative, are of necessity expressed in human words and interpreted by the discursive activity of human minds, and thus share in the inevitable imperfection and incompleteness of all our finite speech and thought, the truth itself (the 'substance of the doctrine' as distinct from its 'formulation') exists in its fullness in the mind of Christ, not as a set of propositions explored by the discursive reason but as one totally apprehended object of the intellect, possessed in all its fullness in one supreme contemplative act. It is because the Church, of which the theologian is a member and an agent, is Christ's body that the formulations are genuine, though partial and inadequate, projections, on to the plane of temporal existence of the Church militant, of the unformulated substance of Christian truth held in the mind of him who is Truth itself. It is in this way that I would solve the problem of the relation between the immutable substance of Christian doctrine and the mutability or unfinished character of its verbal expression.

Once the embellishments have been pared away, what Mascall seems to be saying could be expressed in the following propositions:

> (i) The 'substance of the doctrine' is to be found in the mind of Christ alone.
> (ii) The Church's formulations are genuine (though inadequate and incomplete) because the Church is the Body of Christ.
> (iii) The theologian is a member and agent of the Church.
> (iv) The theologian will be loyal to the substance of the doctrine by cultivating a loyal submission to Christian tradition.

As far as (i) is concerned, even on the most liberal interpretation, Mascall can hardly be wanting us to draw the obvious conclusion that Christ alone can know what the substance of the doctrine is, for if this were literally true then neither Mascall nor any one else could know whether or not any particular analysis of Christian belief (including Mascall's own analysis) was a reductionist analysis, unless of course in some way he had access to the mind of Christ himself. But perhaps Mascall is wanting to hold that the Church, being Christ's body, does, in some sense, have access to the mind of Christ, and that therefore so also does the theologian insofar as the latter is a member and agent of the Church (ii). In which case this suggests that every analysis of the nature of Christian belief which comes from outside the Church is bound to be reductionist because only by being a member of the body of Christ can one have access to the mind of Christ where alone the substance of the doctrine (as distinct from its human verbal formulations) is to be found. But whether or not Mascall is wanting to maintain this dubious position we are still of course left with no criterion for identifying reductionist analyses which are produced from within the Church. For even if it is true (and this would certainly need to be demonstrated) that membership of the Church of the Christ is a necessary condition for producing a non-reductionist analysis of Christian doctrine, it can hardly be a sufficient condition. If it were, Mascall would be faced with the dilemma either of denying that people like Braithwaite, van Buren and Bishop Robinson are really members of the Church (a step which he does not seem willing to take) or else of denying that the analyses of Christian belief produced by these thinkers are 'reductionist' analyses after all. Clearly then, Mascall has some further conditions in mind the fulfilling of which is necessary if 'reductionism' is to be avoided, and this is what, I think, is being alluded to in the fourth of the above propositions, viz. that "the theologian will be loyal to the substance of the doctrine by cultivating a loyal submission to Christian tradition". It is charitable to suppose that this claim is intended to be more than simply a vague exhortation to theological conservatism, but it is far from clear what more than this it could be. For, if one's concern is to give an analysis of the nature of Christian belief in terms of a contemporary philosophical outlook, then being loyally submissive to Christian *tradition* (as distinct from being loyally submissive to Christian *doctrine*) must surely mean something like refusing to depart from *the traditional verbal formulations* of the doctrine. But clearly, not only would this limitation ipso facto render any *contemporary* expression of the doctrines impossible (except insofar as the traditional expression was also the contemporary one) but it would also seem to come close to identifying the substance of the doctrine with its traditional verbal formulations, an identification that is one of the very things which Mascall set out to deny.[7] I conclude therefore that making this distinction intelligible is a much more difficult task than Mascall would lead one to expect, and certainly his own suggestions as to how it might be done, far from pointing to a solution to the problem, either beg the central question at issue or simply render the alleged distinction all the more baffling and obscure.

Another recent attack on 'reductionist' analyses of Christian doctrine has come from Hugo Meynell, whose book *Sense, Nonsense and Christianity*[8] Mascall more than once refers to with warm approval. Like Mascall, Meynell's sympathies are with Catholic-traditionalist interpretations of Christianity and he therefore devotes a whole chapter to examining "reductionist theologies", classical examples of which he finds in the religious writings of Kant, Schleiermacher and Hegel. He sees the presuppositions of these reductionist analyses underlying much of the theology of more recent times. His criterion for distinguishing reductionist from non-reductionist theologies is that the latter include assent to statements of past (historical) and future (eschatological) fact as belonging to the essence of Christian belief, whereas the former regard such statements as more or less dispensable. In other words, for the reductionist, assent to the 'factual' statements will be thought necessary only insofar as they serve as oblique expressions of religious experience, or moral attitudes or existential self-understanding. For the traditionalist on the other hand the factual statements are not merely the *vehicle* of religious and moral experience but their *ground*. Unless the factual statements are true, the experience and attitudes associated with assent to such statements are either inappropriate or unjustified.

There are two points I want to make here. Firstly there is certainly something to be said for regarding as 'reductionist' any analysis of Christian belief which claims that the truth of Christianity is logically independent of the truth of all historical beliefs. Though in any extended treatment of the subject this point would need to be made out, there is, I believe, an enormously powerful prima facie case for the view that it is precisely this logical dependence of specifically religious beliefs on certain historical beliefs which distinguishes Christianity from most, or perhaps all, of the other major world religions, and therefore any analysis of Christianity which obscures or denies this dependence will be, in that respect, misleading and perhaps incipiently reductionist. Of course, insistence on this essential historicity of Christian religious belief involves some well-known difficulties associated with the notion of religious commitment, difficulties which have been recognised at least since the time of Lessing and whose importance I believe is somewhat underestimated by Mascall.[9] But with this topic I am not at present concerned.

My second point concerning Meynell's criterion for identifying reductionism is more critical. Though he justifiably insists that the truth of the Christian religion is logically dependent on the truth of certain historical statements, he seriously oversimplifies the problem of discovering what is the minimal set of historical claims to which the Christian believer is logically committed. For example, he argues that some of the claims made in the Apostle's Creed are either historical statements or imply such statements. The belief that Jesus was conceived by the Holy Ghost, for instance, implies that he was not conceived by any man. The belief that on the third day he rose again implies the belief that the tomb in which he was buried was subsequently empty; and the belief that he ascended into heaven implies the belief that he "disappeared (went up into a cloud?) and was never seen again in circumstances at all similar."[10] Though I think it is clear that none of the clauses of the Apostle's creed just referred to is strictly speaking an historical statement and that each of them nevertheless implies (or as I should prefer to put it) either entails, or presupposes, a historical statement, it is certainly a matter of dispute whether the respective historical statements so entailed or presupposed are the ones which Meynell mentions. In other words, though for example it may be plausibly argued that an interpretation of the Resurrection belief which is logically independent of any historical claim whatever is properly to be regarded as reductionist, to claim that the belief in the Resurrection of Jesus necessarily implies belief in an empty tomb is to beg a great many questions concerning the precise logical status of this belief which are not settled simply by admitting the belief to have, so to speak, an historical core. Of course, if any historical beliefs are entailed then they must be specifiable. But to specify which historical statements are entailed and then to use the acceptance or rejection of these statements as the criterion for distinguishing reductionist from non-reductionist theologies is to have answered in advance the very question which any philosophical analysis of religious beliefs is concerned to investigate, viz. "What is the logical status of these beliefs?", and this will include investigating *which* historical statements are entailed by them. Admittedly, even to assume that the beliefs in question entail or presuppose any historical statements is, strictly speaking, to make certain assumptions concerning the logical status of these beliefs, and I have already suggested that in an extended treatment of the topic these assumptions would certainly have to be justified. But there is some excuse for regarding as 'reductionist' any analysis of Christian beliefs which denies that any of them entails historical statements, because if this denial were justified, the logical status of these beliefs would be almost *totally* different from what appearances would suggest. But to specify which historical statements are entailed by pointing to those which are prima facie entailed, and then to make the acceptance or rejection of *these* statements the criterion for identifying reductionism, is to assume that the prima facie logical status of religious beliefs is *identical* with their actual logical status, But as the question "What is the real (and not merely the apparent) logical status of religious or theological propositions?" is perhaps the central question to ask in any philosophical analysis of belief, Meynell's criterion for distinguishing reductionist from non-reductionist analyses obviously begs the central question at issue.

Secular/humanist attacks on 'reductionism"

So far I have suggested that attacks on so-called reductionism from the standpoint of orthodox/traditionalist Christianity, such as those by Mascall and Meynell, tend to beg the central questions at issue by the very way in which they formulate their criterion for identifying reductionist analyses. I want to argue now that a similar question-begging tendency can be detected in some typical attacks from the side of 'secular-humanism'. Again I shall select two examples to illustrate my point.

R. W. Hepburn in his article 'From World to God' (*Mind*, January 1963), argued that what he calls "belief in the cosmological relation" is essential to Christian belief and that all analyses which bypass such a belief, or interpret it in terms of "attitude commending", or as evocative of a "way of looking at the world" are in fact reductionist analyses. By the "cosmological relation" Hepburn means "the relation between world and God, that relation on which the Cosmological Argument turns."[11] He argues that the belief in the cosmological relation is logically demanded by that strand in Christian discourse in which God is accorded the status of an individual, "the kind of being who may be encountered, who acts and sends his son, and who, because he is capable of doing such things, is therefore not identifiable with ways of seeing phenomena or with attitudes taken up to phenomena"[12]. Hepburn therefore regards as 'reductionist' any analysis which bypasses the 'cosmological relation', or *interprets its logical status as being other than what, on the face of it, it seems to be.*

Nevertheless he admits, or rather insists, that there is also much in Christian discourse which logically demands that

God must not be thought of as an individual to whom the cosmos stands in this relation of quasi-factual dependence. He sees this as evidence of a fundamental contradiction in Christian discourse.

But here again, what I want to ask is why it is not also possible for this same evidence to be interpreted as pointing to a faulty analysis of the logical status of the so-called 'belief in the cosmological relation'. This alternative way of interpreting the evidence may of course turn out to be less plausible – or, on the other hand, *more* plausible. *Which* it is will have to be *shown*, and this will involve a careful and patient investigation of that strand in Christian discourse which seems to point to a belief in the 'cosmological relation' to see whether its actual logical status is, or is not, identical with what it appears to be. In other words, my objection to Hepburn is that he classifies as 'reductionist' any analysis which suggests that this belief in the cosmological relation has anything other than its prima facie logical status, and then observes that when interpreted along non-reductionist lines this belief is both demanded by, and incompatible with, Christian discourse taken as a whole. Surely an equally reasonable and less question-begging conclusion to draw would be that the evidence from Christian discourse taken as a whole suggests that the logical status of the belief in question is other than what, on the face of it, it appears to be. But even if, on careful investigation this should turn out not to be so, then it will only be after such an investigation and not before, that we shall be in a position to apply the term 'reductionist'.

A. C. Macintyre is another philosopher from the 'secular/humanist' camp who has levelled the charge of reductionism at some contemporary interpreters of Christianity, including Bishop Robinson, Tillich, Bultmann and Bonhoeffer.[13] He accuses Tillich (for example) of evacuating belief in God of all its traditional content and so conceding the substance of atheism without being willing to give up a theistic vocabulary. Again he believes Bultmann's theology leads logically to atheism, and Bonhoeffer's outline for a theology points to a way of life, outside the specific context of the concentration camp, that is indistinguishable from that of sensitive generous liberals.

These charges may well turn out to be justified and I certainly do not wish to defend the theological systems of any of these writers. My purpose, however, is to draw attention to MacIntyre's tacit assumption that we all know what the substance of theistic belief is, and that furthermore we know it to be of the essence of Christianity. Though there is a verbal and superficial sense in which this is true, the theologians in question were all of course attempting to show in some deeper sense what belief in God means, and in particular, what it means within the context of the Christian faith as it finds expression in twentieth century secular society. They may well have failed in this attempt, and they certainly have failed to express themselves with even the minimum degree of clarity which we have a right to expect, notwithstanding the difficulty of their subject matter. But to claim that what they have produced is indistinguishable from atheism is to assume that we already know, in this deeper sense, what theism is. It is to assume, that is, that what they were trying to do was in a sense unnecessary.

That the success of MacIntyre's implied charge of reductionism depends on this same question-begging manoeuvre already detected in other writers is further illustrated by his attempt to place on the horns of a dilemma all such theologians who attempt to translate the language of Christian theism for a secular, atheistic world.

> They are doomed to one of two failures. Either they succeed in their translation: in which case what they find themselves saying has been transformed into the

> atheism of their hearers. Or they fail in their translation: in which case no one hears what they have to say but themselves.[14]

This quotation expresses a point of view which frequently underlies the thinking of secular/humanist critics who have brought the charge of reductionism against contemporary analyses of Christian belief – a point of view which might be described as "secular Tertullianism", i.e. not "I believe the Christian Faith because it is absurd," but its corollary, "If it is not absurd it cannot be the Christian faith." If theistic talk is *necessarily* unintelligible to atheists then of course any analysis of theism which *makes sense* to atheists will necessarily be reductionist. The question-begging nature of this working criterion for the detection of reductionism scarcely needs to be further explicated.

Reductionism and the theology/meta-theology distinction

Having now suggested that some of the ways in which the notion of reductionism has been employed have been seriously question-begging, whether at the hands of orthodox/traditionalist defenders of Christian belief or its secular/humanist critics, it is now time to raise the question whether the charge of reductionism is viable at all in the philosophy of religion, and if it is, in what sense. I am well aware that, so far, I have done little more than sketch a case against the four writers concerned, in the course of which a number of concepts have been used, and issues raised, which are in urgent need of further clarification before the argument can be given any degree of rigour. In the remainder of this article I shall do little more than indicate what I think are the fuzziest areas in the argument, and make a few tentative suggestions as to how they might be given a firmer outline.

Perhaps the question in most urgent need of attention is "What is it for something to count as an analysis of Christian belief?", for unless we have a reasonably clear answer to this question we shall not be in a position to discover what it is for something to count as a *reductionist* analysis. It might be argued, for example, that we need to distinguish between an analysis of Christian belief and that of the *nature* of Christian belief, or, as some might prefer to put it, between the first-order enquiry commonly referred to as theology, and the second-order enquiry of meta-theology which (according to some) is what the philosophy of religion should properly be understood to be.[15]

On the basis of this distinction between first- and second-order enquiries, G. E. Hughes has raised the question whether a reductionist meta-theology is necessarily incompatible with an orthodox theology. He asks,

> Must one hold an orthodox meta-theology before one can be said to subscribe to an orthodox theology? Indeed, is there (could there be) an orthodox meta-theology; or are there only orthodox doctrines, not orthodox doctrines about doctrines?[16]

These remarks occur in the context of Hughes's critical notice of C. B. Martin's book *Religious Belief*, in which Martin rejects reductionist theories of the Braithwaitean type on the grounds that most Christians would reject them as being inadequate accounts of what belief in Christian doctrines comes to. "But," says Hughes,

> how good is this as a reason? Are the users of a certain type of language always the best judges of the adequacy of a philosophical account of what precisely the function of that language is? The phenomenalist in epistemology or the emotivist in ethics is likely to be unmoved by the fact (if it is a fact) that most users of material object language or moral language are unsympathetic to his account. And rightly, surely?[17]

Here two different but connected difficulties obviously arise. Firstly, can the distinction between theology and meta-theology be sustained in any systematic way, and secondly, even if it can, by what criteria do we judge any particular meta-theology to be an adequate account of its related first-order discipline?

There are certainly formidable problems to be overcome in connection with the theology/meta-theology distinction. Though we *can* distinguish between *using* the concepts God, holy, salvation, eternal life, sin, etc. on the one hand, and discussing and analysing them on the other, this distinction will not I think take us very far in grappling with the problem of identifying reductionism, for much of what commonly falls under the heading of theology, which is supposed to be the first-order enquiry, consists of the systematic and even critical analysis, discussion and explication of theological terms. For example any respectable (or, if you like, respected) book on Christian theology will devote whole chapters to describing what Christians understand by the concepts of God, the Trinity, sin, salvation, atonement, etc. I don't think that what this means is that many books commonly taken to be on theology are really mostly on the philosophy of religion. What it does mean is that the distinction between the two disciplines cannot usefully be drawn simply by reference to the difference between first- and second-order levels of discourse. In practice I think it will be related more closely to questions of commitment and detachment, though of course this latter aspect is not unrelated to the distinction I have been discussing.

But even if the theology/meta-theology distinction *can* be shown to be a viable one, by what criteria are we to decide the extent to which any given meta-theology provides an adequate account of the nature of religious belief? The difficulty in answering this question, considerable as it is, has I believe been unnecessarily aggravated by confusing it with the question which forms the sub-title of this article. I shall now try to justify this remark.

Supposing someone were to maintain that if an analysis of· religious belief is in fact reductionist then it is *necessarily* inadequate. This might mean that he is using the word "reductionist" in such a way that "inadequate" was part of its meaning, so for him the proposition "All reductionist analyses are inadequate" would be analytic. When the word is used in this way it has a negative evaluative element as part of its meaning, and it is the *content* of religious belief which is thought of as having been 'reduced' or eviscerated. I shall call this sense of "reductionism" R1. Alternatively however, the person might be wanting to maintain (when claiming that reductionist analyses are necessarily inadequate) that religious language is in some sense sui generis, and that therefore the nature of religious belief is not adequately expressible or even explicable in terms which are themselves entirely non-religious. When the word is used in this way attention is focussed on the linguistic vehicle in which the content of belief is conveyed, and what is primarily being asserted is perhaps roughly analogous to what is being asserted by the non-naturalist in ethical theory. This sense of "reductionism" I shall call R2. Now it seems likely that some of the objections to so-called reductionist analyses have confused or conflated these two ways of using the term in such a way as to obscure the kind of justification which is demanded of anyone who describes a piece of analysis as 'reductionist'. For if a piece of analysis is described as R1-reductionist then all that this amounts to is that it is judged to be inadequate in some way, and this charge of course would have to be justified by some sort of argument. Now one such argument might be to show that the analysis is an attempt to express the nature of religious belief in terms which are entirely non-religious, i.e. to show that the analysis is R2-reductionist. But then for this to count as a justification it would be necessary in turn to justify the thesis that religious language is sui generis in the required sense. It may of course be possible to prove this thesis, though as far as I am aware no one has yet done this, nor am I at all clear how one would set about doing it. What I suspect tends to happen though is that once a piece of analysis is diagnosed as R2-reductionist it is assumed, ipso facto, to be inadequate, simply because the negative evaluative element in R1 tends to be conflated with the purely descriptive content of R2.

All this suggests that the concept of reductionism cannot be used as a criterion for judging the extent to which any given analysis (meta-theological or otherwise) provides an adequate account of the nature of religious beliefs unless it is supplemented by a body of theory which explains what are the logical connections between 'reductionism' and 'inadequacy'. I am not of course claiming that such a body of theory *could not* be supplied, but simply that for the most part it *has not* been supplied by those who have most frequently employed the concept, and as a consequence there has been a tendency to beg some of the fundamental questions at issue, as I tried to show in the earlier part of this article. In particular it might be worth working out in detail whether or not there is any close analogy between anti-naturalism in ethics and the view that religious language is in some sense *sui generis*, a question that certainly cannot be answered simply by an appeal to what has been called the idiosyncratic platitude, viz. "Every mode of discourse has its own logic".

Notes

1. London, 1965.
2. Mascall criticised Braithwaite's Eddington Memorial Lecture at greater length in his *Words and Images* (London, 1957).

3. *The Secularisation of Christianity*, p. 36.
4. Bishop Robinson himself, however, seems to share Mascall's confidence in the possibility of distinguishing the 'truth' of the doctrine from its linguistic expression. It is his conviction that whereas the latter is a matter of doubt and controversy, the former is something to which he has an unreserved commitment. Cf. "I have never really doubted the fundamental truth of the Christian faith – though I have constantly found myelf questioning its expression." (*Honest to God*, p. 27).
5. *The Secularisation of Christianity*, p. 36.
6. *The Secularisation of Christianity*, pp. 36–38.
7. It is not disputed that a knowledge of Christian tradition is essential to a proper understanding of Christian belief, but clearly Mascall's claim is much stronger than this.
8. London, 1964.
9. The difficulties alluded to are pungently discussed in chapters VI and VII of R. W. Hepburn's *Christianity and Paradox* (London, 1958).
10. *The Secularisation of Christianity*, p. 56.
11. 'From World to God', p. 42.
12. 'From World to God', pp. 40–41.
13. 'God and the Theologians', *Encounter*, September 1963 (repr. with abbreviations in *The Honest to God Debate*, ed. D. L. Edwards and J. A. T. Robinson, London 1963).
14. 'God and the Theologians.'
15. See, for example, J. Hick, *Philosophy of Religion* (New York, 1963), Introduction, p. 1.
16. *The Australian Journal of Philosophy*, 1962, p. 217.
17. Ibid.

Postscript

This paper was originally read at a Philosophy of Religion conference held in Australia in 1964 or 1965. Among those attending was Professor Richard Hare trom Oxford University, a distinguished scholar principally in the field of moral philosophy. He was also a significant contributor to the philosophy of religion. When I learned that he was to be present at the conference I was extremely apprehensive and very nearly decided to withdraw my paper. It seemed to me not to be of sufficient merit to be worth presenting at a conference attended by philosophers of Hare's calibre.

However, following the reading of my paper, Hare approached me in private and, to my surprise, made some highly complimentary comments. Consequently, I offered the paper to the editors of the Australian journal *Sophia* who subsequently published it in the issue of October, 1966, vol. V, no. 3. Hare repeated the compliment in print in an essay entitled 'The Simple Believer' (published in *Religion and Morality*, ed. G. Outka and J.P. Reeder, Anchor Press, 1973). In reference to the style of question-begging argument of the kind I attacked in my paper he remarked ". . . an entirely devastating rebuttal of it has already been given by Mr J.C. Thornton in his article 'Religious Belief and Reductionism'".

Unfortunately, the editors of *Sophia* had not given me an opportunity to correct the proofs, and so the article appeared in print littered with errors (most of which I have now corrected). It evoked a reply by E.L. Mascall, Professor of Philosophy at King's College, London, which was published in *Sophia*, July 1967, vol. VI, no.2, together with my response.

Theological Reductionism

E . L. Mascall

May I make a few comments on Mr. J. C. Thornton's very helpful discussion in *Sophia*, October 1966, of my criticism of theological 'reductionism'?

I agree that no formulation in human language can precisely and exhaustively reproduce the content of the truth that is possessed in its fulness in the mind of Christ. Furthermore no two formulations in human language are likely to have precisely the same significance, since the meaning of each is dependent on its cultural context; even the same formulation may not carry precisely the same meaning to two different people, since each of them has his own context in which he places it. As I said, even "The cat is black" and "Le chat est noir" may not carry precisely the same meaning to two hearers. Nevertheless two sentences can be equivalent in all relevant respects, otherwise communication by language would be impossible. "The cat is black" and "Le chat est noir" can be legitimately described as equivalent in a sense in which it would not be legitimate to describe either as equivalent to "The cow is purple". Mr. Thornton seems to me to fall into the fallacy which, because there are organisms about which it is difficult to know whether they are animals or plants, refuses to admit that a cedar is a plant or an elephant an animal. I cannot see how by any legitimate process it is possible to interpret "Jesus was born of the Virgin Mary" as equivalent to "Jesus was born of the non-virgin Mary but was a person of unique significance", or, with Dr. Boslooper, as equivalent to "God has acted in history and monogamous marriage is civilisation's most important social institution". If this was what the Creed meant it would have been perfectly able to say it. Admittedly some theological statements contain a metaphorical or analogical element, when the event or object which they are describing inherently transcends our normal experience. Thus, "He came down from heaven" has never been taken by theologians as referring to a local movement, since God does not occupy a limited volume of space but is, in one respect, not in space at all and is, in another respect, everywhere. An equally transcendent character attaches to "He became man", and the *Quicunque vult* glosses this with the words "not by the conversion of godhead into flesh but by assumption of manhood into God".

"He rose from the dead" raises some important and special questions. To take it as meaning "His disciples had an 'Easter experience'", with the suggestion that nothing happened to Jesus at all, is, I would claim, a clear misuse of words; but what are we to say about the interpretation "His soul survived and was transformed", with the suggestion that his body remained and mouldered in the tomb? This appears to be the interpretation favoured by Dr. Lampe in a recently published pamphlet (G. W. H. Lampe and D. M. MacKinnon, *The Resurrection*, London 1966). According to him, St. Paul did not believe in the bodily resurrection of Jesus but the primitive Church embroidered a purely spiritual "resurrection" with the myth of the empty tomb. It is here that the question of context is relevant in deciding the "meaning" of the credal statement. *Pace* Dr. Lampe, it seems clear that what the primitive Church was anxious to affirm was the survival and transformation of Jesus in the totality of his humanity and that Jesus' resurrection was an anticipation and a "first fruit" of the future resurrection to which Christians look forward themselves. Behind this lies the conviction that the material element in man and the universe at large will be glorified and assumed into Christ. *Pace* Dr. Quick again, this seems to me to be clearly what St. Paul has in mind in I Corinthians xv. Thus I would say that, while the statement "He rose from the dead", when made in the context of the Christian religion, is not equivalent to "The tomb was empty", it certainly includes and presupposes it. What I hold to be objectionable in the type of 'reductionism' that I have criticised is not that it 'reinterprets' or 'translates' the traditional formulae, but (i) that it removes them altogether from the context in which they were born, and (ii) that it tries to justify this process by alleging that what the primitive Church 'really meant' was something that it clearly did not mean in any normal sense of meaning and which it would have been well able to express in ordinary words if it had in fact meant it.

On a different issue raised by Mr. Thornton, I do not hold that membership of the Church (in the sense of full and visible membership) is either a necessary or a sufficient condition for producing a non-reductionist analysis of Christian doctrine. But, since the formulations which are subjected to analysis have been produced within the context of the life and thought of the Church, the meaning which any legitimate restatement must preserve can hardly be discerned without an attempt to enter imaginatively into that context; this is only one example of a principle that holds in any work of intelligent literary criticism. And the most obvious way to enter into that context is to be living and seeking to understand the life of the Church itself. A Christian will also presumably attach some significance to the guidance by the Spirit which Jesus promised to his body the Church. My charge against the 'reductionists' is that, although many of them are members of the Church, in their interpretation of the Church's formulae they do their thinking not in the context of the Church but in a context of an entirely secular culture. Their secularist critics seem to me to have a perfectly good point when they complain that the reductionists simply cloud the issue by using the traditional formulae with meanings that they cannot reasonably bear, and that they are (to change the metaphor) trying to run with the hare and follow with the hounds.

I am only too ready to admit the difficulty and delicacy of the task of interpreting the traditional beliefs without distorting them; it needs much more work than I have been able to do upon it. But I am sure that it is not to be done by making a guess at what the contemporary secular thinker is prepared to swallow and then cooking the Christian answers into the corresponding shape.

Reductionism: a reply to Dr. Mascall

J. C. Thornton

I am grateful to Dr. Mascall for his (on the whole) sympathetic comments on my article, but I feel he has largely missed the point I was trying to make. In particular I do not think that I am guilty of having committed the fallacy he mentions. I take it that, by his analogy, he is suggesting that the nub of my argument was as follows:

> Because it is sometimes difficult to distinguish between the substance of a doctrine and its formulation we are never in a position to say which is which.

However, this was not my argument. An examination of *Sophia* (Oct. 1966), pp. 3–8, will I believe show that what I was saying was that if the distinction between the "substance" of a doctrine and its "verbal formulation" is to be used as a basis for identifying reductionist analyses of Christian belief then the task of showing what the distinction is (i.e. making it intelligible) is more difficult than Dr. Mascall would lead one to expect, and I tried to show that his own suggestions as to how it might be done are quite unsatisfactory. Far from regarding the distinction in question as hopelessly unintelligible, however, I myself would agree that some such distinction has to be made whenever there is any attempt to express Christianity in "contemporary terms". The point I was making was simply that it is fatally easy to oversimplify this distinction in ways which inevitably lead to the setting up of arbitrary and question-begging criteria for the detecting of reductionism.

In particular, I would argue that the relationship between the "substance" and the "verbal formulation" of a religious doctrine is a much more complex one than that between what is normally spoken of as the "meaning" of a sentence and the sentence itself. Yet Mascall's use of the examples "The cat is black" and "Le chat est noir", etc. strongly suggest that this is the distinction which, in his judgment, is basically the one involved. Admittedly he hints that the matter is more complicated in the case of "some theological statements (which) contain a metaphorical or analogical element, when the event or object which they are describing inherently transcends our normal experience," but the impression remains that in his view the substance/formulation relationship is fundamentally the meaning/sentence relationship.

Without at this stage developing the point, I would argue that these two relationships are vastly different unless "meaning" is used in an extremely broad sense, in which case the meaning/sentence relationship becomes no more illuminating than the substance/formulation relationship. At the risk of some over-simplification I would suggest that when someone asks, "What is the substance (as distinct from the verbal formulation) of the doctrines contained in the so-called Nicene Creed?" then if he can be said to be asking for the "meaning" of these doctrines he is not asking for it in the same sense of "meaning" as when someone ignorant of Latin asks, "What is the meaning of 'Credo in unum Deum'?".

Anyone who can translate the words of the Nicene Creed from Latin into English in one perfectly straightforward sense *knows* the meaning of the Latin sentences which go to make up the Creed (and, incidentally, not merely the meanings of the Latin words which go to make up the sentences). But, of course, it does not follow either that he can say, or even that he knows, what is the "substance" of the credal doctrines in the sense presumably conveyed by that word (whatever precisely that may be) when used by both Pope Paul and Dr. Mascall himself in the sentence "The substance of the ancient deposit of faith is one thing; its verbal formulation quite another." Therefore, whatever is meant by "substance" here it is not "meaning" in the same sense as in "The meaning of 'Le chat est noir' is 'The cat is black.'"

Nor is this point really affected by appealing to the "metaphorical or analogical element" contained in some theological statements when the event or object which they are describing "inherently transcends our normal experience". It is of course true that a difficulty sometimes arises in translating idiomatic, figurative or analogical expressions from one language into another. But this is only part – and perhaps not even the most important part – of the difficulty of determining what the substance of a theological doctrine is. Otherwise we would expect the latter kind of difficulty to disappear once one had become thoroughly acquainted with the language in which the doctrine is expressed. But this is not what we find. It is well known that scholars whose familiarity with the relevant languages is undisputed may nevertheless differ sharply concerning what they judge to be the substance of a theological doctrine.

It is clear then that if to ask for the substance of a doctrine is to ask for its meaning, then "meaning" is being used in a much wider sense than in the sentence "The meaning of 'Le chat est noir' is 'The cat is black'". It will of course certainly be relevant to take into account matters of cultural context, etc. (quite properly mentioned by Dr. Mascall) in order to discover what is ordinarily spoken of as the "meaning" of a doctrine, but also in order to discover what is not normally included under that term but which may nevertheless be considered part of a doctrine's "meaning" in an extended sense, viz. such matters as the nature and purpose of the linguistic or speech acts performed by the formulators of the doctrine. Indeed, only by paying attention to the possible varieties of speech acts (such as are explored in J. L. Austin's *How to do Things with Words* [Oxford, 1962]), as well as to what is ordinarily referred to as the "meaning" of a sentence will there be much hope of distinguishing those aspects of the doctrines which are of permanent importance and value from those which are ephemeral, incidental or even mistaken. If, as I suspect, the making of some such distinction as this is what is essentially involved in identifying the substance of a doctrine in any intelligible sense, then the setting up of criteria for making the distinction will necessarily be far more complicated, controversial and even subjective than it would seem Dr. Mascall is prepared to recognise.

3

Determinism and Moral Reactive Attitudes

It has frequently been observed that the real difficulty of the problem of free will and determinism is not answering the question "Are our wills free or determined?" but discovering whether or not this is the right question to ask. The primary difficulty lies in properly formulating the problem, for unless it is properly formulated the efforts made to solve it will be vitiated from the start. Thus the question "Are our wills free or determined?" would generally be agreed to be not one of the happiest of philosophical questions, partly because of the obscurity of the terms "will," "free," and "determined," and partly because this very obscurity renders the implied opposition between the last two terms highly question-begging.

Not that vague terms cannot be made more precise. The real difficulty is that it is not clear which ways of making their meanings more precise are the relevant ways, or even what the appropriate procedure would be for finding this out. By way of contrast, consider the unphilosophical question, "Is education in New Zealand free or compulsory?" – a question we can imagine being asked by a foreign academic (perhaps not perfectly familiar with the idioms of the English language) who is considering taking up a university appointment in New Zealand. Here again we might agree that the question is not very happily formulated. The key terms "education," "free," and "compulsory" are all vague or ambiguous, but they can all be made more precise and relatively unequivocal. Moreover, there is little doubt concerning what would be the relevant ways of doing this. We could point out that education in New Zealand is compulsory in the sense that all children between the ages of seven and fifteen are required by law to attend an approved educational institution. Though, therefore, 'not voluntary', education is nevertheless 'free' in the sense that most of the cost of it is paid indirectly through taxation rather than directly in the form of school fees. Education of the formal sort appropriate to children in the above-mentioned age group is therefore both 'compulsory' and (in a sense) 'free', so that the opposition implied in the original formulation of the question is an unreal one. Can the question about free will be handled in a similar way? Ever since the seventeenth century, and perhaps even before that, there have been some philosophers who have thought that it can. Basically, their method has been to give some sort of coherent meaning to the term "will," clarify the senses in which it can be said to be 'free' and 'determined', respectively, and then declare, sometimes triumphantly, that there is no contradiction in insisting that the will is both free and determined, and that therefore the opposition implied in the original formulation of the question is an unreal one. Unfortunately, no philosopher has yet been able to do this with anything like the success which we can imagine might well attend the analogous handling of the question about education in New Zealand. This is not just because the terms involved are so much more obscure but rather because it is not easy to see that there would necessarily be any agreement concerning the relevant way in which they can be made more precise. With the question about education being asked by someone who was considering whether or not to travel to New Zealand to settle, we can have a fair idea of the sort of considerations which would weigh with anyone faced with the responsibility of having their children educated in a new country. The practical considerations guide us in the way we go about clarifying the concepts and keep us from considering all these possible meanings which would obviously be irrelevant to that sort of context which the question might reasonably be expected to have. For example, we would not normally go into the question of whether education in New Zealand was free in the sense of being 'loose' or 'unfettered' or 'unrestrained' or 'spontaneous' or 'informal', though contexts could no doubt be found in which it would be appropriate to describe education in New Zealand (either truly or falsely) as being 'free' in each of these senses. The baffling nature of the question about free will and determinism is, at least in part, due to the fact that it is enormously difficult to be sure which attempts at clarifying the concepts involved we can agree are the relevant ones. Consequently, it is common for philosophers who have written on what they have taken to be the problem of free will to be accused by others of completely begging the question. In spite of all the clarifying of concepts and the resolving of apparent contradictions, it is complained that the central problem has been neatly sidestepped.

This sort of situation, common in discussions of free will, arises perhaps because what appears to one as the central problem does not necessarily so appear to another. And even if, as would seem more sensible, we speak of a cluster of problems, which of the problems are seen to be the more urgent will be a matter of varied opinion. With the question about education in New Zealand, the relatively specific nature of the sort of context in which the question might be meaningfully asked, and the sharing of a common concern with such relatively down-to-earth matters as the cost, nature, and scope of a nation's educational system ensure that the necessary clarifying of the terms will proceed along lines fairly readily accepted by all as being the relevant ones. But with a question as wide in its scope as the question of free will and determinism, there is no relatively specific practical concern to guide the direction of our clarifying analysis.

It might be objected at this point that, on the contrary, there is the practical concern with morality to provide this directional guide, for by far the majority of discussions concerning free will and determinism have been centered around the concept of moral responsibility. If many of us are concerned with the way our children are educated and how much it will cost us, surely all of us (or at least all of us interested in philosophy) are concerned with whether or not the truth of determinism would entail that morality is a farce and the notions of guilt, blame, and moral responsibility are inherently confused. Won't this fundamental, common, practical concern ensure that our attempts to come to grips with the problem proceed along lines which are agreed to be relevant (even though there might be plenty of disagreement concerning the degree of progress made)?

So it would seem. But I suspect that what is at the root of the trouble, and perhaps goes further than we might expect toward accounting for some of the frustrations and the mutual accusations of question-begging, is the existence of differences in moral outlook. I am not thinking so much now of differences in moral judgment typified, for example, in such questions as that of capital punishment, pacifism, or gambling. I have in mind the more subtle variations from one individual to another concerning what is felt to be the relative importance of moral dispositional attitudes such as resentment, forgiveness, shame, and remorse, as well as the less intimately personal attitudes such as public spirit and the concern for social justice. It is obvious that we are not all equally sensitive at the pressure points of interpersonal relationships with which these moral dispositional attitudes are associated, but it is less obvious that the relative degrees of sensitivity in these attitudes, or rather the way the pattern of degrees of sensitivity displayed in the attitude complex varies from one individual to another, bear no direct relation to our judgment concerning an individual's moral worth. We admire Tom for his outward-going benevolence, his relative indifference to the opinions which others have of him, his capacity for good humour at his own expense, his reliability and cheerfulness. We admire Dick for his deep sensitivity to the feelings of others, for his courtesy and his quiet integrity. We admire Harry for his dedicated sense of service to the wider community, for his drive and energy in the pursuit of social justice. Tom, Dick, and Harry are, in different ways, perhaps all equally good men. None of them, of course, is perfect: each has his own peculiar failings. But more significantly, the pattern of dispositional moral attitudes in each is very different. Tom's nature is such that he finds it easy to forgive; Dick often finds it difficult, and the difficulty troubles his conscience for he is sure that he ought to be forgiving; whereas Harry is as uncompromising with others as he is with himself, and his whole manner, if not his speech, thunders forth judgment and retribution as from a prophet in the desert.

Now if Tom, Dick, and Harry should all happen to be philosophers, it will hardly be surprising if they come to different conclusions concerning what consequences the possible truth of determinism would have for moral responsibility. And even if we discount this as being irrelevant on the good grounds that the soundness or otherwise of a philosopher's views are to be judged by examining his arguments rather than his moral attitude, it may well make a difference to a philosopher's thinking on the relation of determinism and moral responsibility if his paradigm of a moral agent is a Tom rather than a Dick, or a Dick rather than a Harry. Furthermore, we can hardly avoid thinking about this subject except from our own point of view as moral agents, so it would seem that not only the sort of conclusions we draw but the very way we formulate the problem, and therefore the very questions we seem to others to be begging, will depend to a considerable degree on whether we happen to be a Tom or Dick or Harry, or (as is more likely) one or another of the whole gamut of (mainly) less worthy characters that make up the phenomenon of man, and of which Tom, Dick, and Harry are but three of the more easily contrasted stereotypes. The point I am trying to make is simply that too little attention has been paid to the considerable range of different ways of being a morally responsible agent, *even at roughly the same level of moral goodness*, and that, consequently, analyses of the problem of free will and moral responsibility which have failed to take this variety into account have inevitably appeared inadequate, or even irrelevant, to those who see moral responsibility, though not necessarily moral goodness, in a different light.

I shall now try to give a firmer outline to the admittedly vague and unsubstantiated claims which I have just made by discussing at some length P. F. Strawson's British Academy lecture 'Freedom and Resentment'[1] which, I believe, in some respects both exemplifies the weakness which I have claimed characterises much contemporary discussion of the problem of free will and moral responsibility, and yet, to a much greater degree, is also highly suggestive of ways in which that same weakness might be remedied. Hence, though I am critical of some points in Strawson's argument, I am convinced that his highly individual approach to the subject by way of a careful and painstaking analysis of our moral dispositional attitudes as displayed in interpersonal relationships is full of promise. Whether he would approve of the particular use which I have made of his arguments is, of course, another matter.

Strawson is concerned to see what implications the possible truth of the thesis of determinism would have for moral responsibility. This is, of course, a well-worn theme, but his approach is untypical in two respects, one negative and the other positive. First, he is not sure what it is, or even whether it can be coherently stated. However, as it is certain that at least some of our beliefs about, and attitudes toward, human behaviour would remain unaffected no matter what the thesis of determinism should turn out to be, Strawson is concerned with showing that included in these beliefs and attitudes are those which are central to our ordinary notions of moral responsibility and that, therefore, there is no need to know exactly what the thesis of determinism is, for whether it should turn out to be true or false, or even radically incoherent, we can know from a consideration of the purely formal possibilities that it will in no way affect our fundamental notions of moral responsibility. Of course, the view that the truth of determinism is quite compatible with our fundamental notions of moral responsibility (the "optimists' view," as Strawson calls it) has been one whose pedigree can be traced back through Nowell-Smith, Mill, Hume, and Hobbes (to name only some of its more vigorous exponents). However, unlike Strawson, all those philosophers thought it an essential part of their task to say, as clearly as possible, just what the thesis of determinism is in order to show why its truth is compatible with (or even a necessary presupposition of) the notion of moral responsibility. However, though they have had little difficulty in showing that the notions of moral praise and blame can function within a deterministic framework (for praise and blame can be seen to be the means by which we bring about socially desirable ends), nevertheless they have been less convincing in showing that the justification they offer for the infliction of punishment, for example, is the right sort of justification. In a word, the optimists have appeared to many to be at their weakest on the notion of moral desert. It is precisely because of this weakness that the "pessimists," as Strawson calls them, have concluded that to let determinism in the door does, after all, mean pushing the central notions of moral responsibility out the window. Some of the pessimists, therefore, have shut both door and window and created the metaphysical fug known as 'contracausal libertarianism', whereas the rest have opened both door and window and braved the cold draft of what William James called 'hard determinism'; that is, they have accepted the thesis of determinism, at the same time admitting its consequent destruction of the central notions of moral responsibility. The 'soft determinists' (Strawson's optimists), in arguing for an open door and shut window, have, in Strawson's view, failed to convert the pessimists, primarily because they have neglected the range of interpersonal attitudes we display in our ordinary dealings with our fellow human beings, attitudes which can be seen to encapsulate the central notions of moral responsibility, attitudes which it would be scarcely conceivable for us to repudiate even in theory, let alone in practice, no matter what theoretical considerations concerning determinism were thought to demand such a repudiation. This direction of our attention to the importance of interpersonal attitudes is the positive feature of Strawson's handling of this hoary problem. His argument is that not only does an analysis of such interpersonal attitudes reveal that the abandonment of them is not for human beings a practical option, but also that it is in these very interpersonal attitudes that we shall find what the pessimists have rightly seen to be missing in the typical optimist's account, namely, the notion of moral desert. If it is to be found here, there will be no need for the libertarians to look for it in metaphysical notions of contra-causal freedom, nor will the hard determinists need to retreat into moral skepticism out of despair of finding a place for it in a deterministic framework.

Strawson's argument, therefore, has two prongs: first, that no conceivable thesis of determinism could be such as to make it 'rational' for us to abandon, or radically modify, our everyday interpersonal moral attitudes in which are embedded the central notions of moral responsibility; second, that we need not look beyond an analysis of such attitudes for an intelligible account of the notion of moral desert.

How does Strawson support the first of these contentions, namely, that the central notions of moral responsibility embedded in our interpersonal moral attitudes are ineradicable? The essence of his argument is as follows:

> We don't feel resentment whenever we suffer harm, but only when we judge the harm to have been unjustifiably inflicted. We don't feel grateful for every benefit we have received but only for those we see to have been benevolently bestowed. But resentment and gratitude are only two of a whole range of interpersonal reactive attitudes. What is characteristic of these attitudes is that they are not simply feelings which the human animal has in reaction to agreeable and disagreeable experiences. Rather, they are feelings whose very quality is dependent upon our moral appraisal of the situation. Show us that our moral appraisal of the situation was in some way mistaken and the feeling is immediately modified or even removed.

Strawson selected 'resentment' for particular attention as it provided him with a useful paradigm of the sort of moral reactive attitude relevant to his argument. It is interesting to notice that somewhat similar observations were made "upon resentment" by Bishop Butler in his sermon of that title. Butler makes the point that it is not mere harm but 'injury' or the threat of injury which provokes resentment, 'injury' being used here in the sense of 'harm unjustly inflicted', which was the common eighteenth-century sense of the word and, incidentally, is still given as the first meaning of the word in the *Oxford English Dictionary*. That this is the true nature of resentment, Butler argues, "is abundantly confirmed by observing what it is which heightens or lessens resentment; namely, the same which aggravates or lessens the fault: friendship, and former obligations, on one hand; or inadvertancy, strong temptations, and mistake, on the other."[2] Similarly, Strawson also refers to the "sorts of special considerations [which] might be expected to modify or mollify this feeling or remove it altogether". These excusing circumstances Strawson divides into two main groups. The first, in which would be included Butler's 'inadvertancy' and 'mistake', are those which invite us to withhold resentment, not because we regard the agent who caused or threatened the harm as being other than a responsible moral agent but because the circumstances in the particular situation were such that a release from moral responsibility for that particular action is called for – as when someone "didn't know" that the man he was criticizing was my personal friend, or when someone treads on my toe in the bus because "he was pushed." But Strawson also considers another class of circumstances in which for a short or long period, or even permanently, we are obliged to regard the agent as being other than fully responsible. This second group includes Butler's "strong temptations" as when someone is said to be "not himself," but also includes another subgroup (not mentioned by Butler) in which the agent is seen to be psychologically abnormal or morally undeveloped. As Strawson puts it, "The agent was himself; but he is warped or deranged, neurotic or just a child. When we see someone in such a light as this all our reactive attitudes tend to be profoundly modified."[4] In cases such as these, he suggests, what is called for is the abandonment of our normal interpersonal attitudes or range of attitudes appropriate to involvement or participation in human relationships and the adoption of some kind of objective attitude. Strawson describes the 'objective attitude' at some length, but essentially it is the sort of attitude adopted when we see another human being as "an object of social policy; as a subject for what, in a wide range of senses, might be called treatment . . . as something to be managed or handled or cured or trained."[5] He is at pains not to oversimplify and does not wish to claim that these opposing attitudes are strictly exclusive of one another, or that they are incapable of being held to a greater or lesser degree. The essential point is that "there is a tension between them and that the adoption of the objective attitude toward a person tends to inhibit, partially or wholly, the normal participant-reactive attitudes of human involvement."

"The question we have to ask," says Strawson, "is: what effect would or should the acceptance of the truth of a general thesis of determinism have upon these reactive attitudes? More specifically, would or should the acceptance of the truth of the thesis lead to the decay or the repudiation of all such attitudes? Would or should it mean the end of gratitude, resentment, forgiveness; of all reciprocated adult loves; of all the essentially *personal* antagonisms?"[6]

Strawson's answer is, in effect, that it neither would nor should mean this and that we can know that this is true without even knowing what the thesis of determinism is. A belief in the truth of determinism would not mean the decay or repudiation of interpersonal attitudes because, as members of the human race, we would be incapable of sustaining a strictly objective attitude toward *all* other human beings at all times, because the personal isolation which this would entail, together with the consequent loss of the esteem, friendship, and love of others on which we depend for our very existence as sane and civilized human beings would be such that to adopt such a permanent, thoroughgoing, comprehensively objective attitude to others would be all but unthinkable. Furthermore, he continues, it could not possibly be rational to adopt such an attitude (no matter what theoretical considerations seemed to demand it) because 'rationality' in this sort of context can only be assessed in the light of an assessment of the enrichment and impoverishment of human life, and there can be little doubt as to which of these alternatives an adoption of a thoroughgoing objective attitude would lead.

What I have given is a summary of that part of Strawson's argument centered around the notion of resentment, though it will be appreciated that much of the effectiveness of his thesis lies in the cumulative strength of his careful qualifications and illuminating examples. Without these, his attempt to bypass the problem of deciding what the thesis of determinism is inevitably appears more question-begging than it really is. Nevertheless, I think it is question-begging all the same, though not quite in the way in which he denies it is. In fact, one might even say that his argument is question-begging in a way which is potentially illuminating and fruitful.

Expressed in the baldest outline, Strawson's argument seems to be this:

> There are various ways in which we *normally* modify or withhold resentment – for example, the agent was ignorant of what he did, or was pushed, or was unduly provoked, or was insane, or only a child, or a moral idiot. But then it cannot be claimed as a consequence of the truth of determinism (whatever that thesis may be) that whenever anyone caused harm to another either he was pushed, or did not know what he was doing, or was unduly provoked, etc., etc. Nor can it be a consequence of the thesis that everyone is a child, or psychologically or morally abnormal. Hence the thesis of determinism (whatever it may be) can provide no grounds for maintaining that it is never logically appropriate to adopt an attitude of resentment. Yet this interpersonal reactive attitude, along with many other

such attitudes, encapsulates our fundamental notions of moral responsibility.

What seems to be assumed in Strawson's argument, and what one would have thought he has no right to assume without begging the question at issue, is that the only way in which an acceptance of determinism could modify or repudiate the attitude of resentment is in one or another of the ways in which the attitude is *normally* modified or repudiated. In other words, it seems to be assumed that there cannot be any other sort of reason for repudiating or modifying the attitude over and above any of the reasons that we already have. But might it not be true that determinism can provide just such an additional sort of reason, a reason which is not just one of the usual reasons in disguise? Furthermore, might it not be true that the particular kind of modification called for on the basis of an acceptance of determinism was of a different sort or at a different logical level from that appropriate to the ordinary reasons of mistake, tender age, idiocy, etc.? Perhaps a negative answer can be given to both of these questions, or maybe they are only pseudo-questions which cannot be given any coherent sense. But if this is so, it will have to be *shown* that it is so, and it is far from clear that Strawson has done this. The impression that is left is that these questions have simply been begged.

I suspect that Strawson's comment at this point would be that he has shown that such questions cannot sensibly be asked by showing that the abandonment of the whole range of moral reactive attitudes in favour of a sustained objectivity of interpersonal attitude is not even a live option for us. "The fact of our natural human commitment to ordinary interpersonal attitudes . . . is part of the general framework of human life, not something that can come up for review as particular cases can come up for review within the general framework."[7] In support of this he argues that in particular cases where we do modify or repudiate attitudes such as resentment, we find that we do so for quite a wide variety of reasons, different reasons being appropriate in different cases. What we never find, he says, is that we have modified or repudiated resentment in a particular case as a consequence of a prior embracing of the belief that the behaviour of the person in question, or the relevant stretch of behavior, was 'determined' in the sense in which, if determinism is true, all behaviour is determined. In other words, in any particular case, the abandoning of the normal interpersonal attitudes in favour of an 'objective attitude' is never from a theoretical conviction that might be expressed as "determinism in this case".[8]

The plausibility of this part of his argument, however, again depends on the assumed argument that if a belief in determinism were to provide us with a good reason for adopting the objective attitude (with the consequent rejection of the moral participant attitudes) toward all human behaviour, it would only be because it was already acknowledged to be a good reason for adopting such an attitude toward some human behaviour. But here again the unwarranted assumption is that either a belief in determinism provides us with a reason for rejecting the participant attitudes which is on the same logical level as reasons such as psychological abnormality, ignorance, undue provocation, etc., or it doesn't provide us with a reason at all. But this is just what would not be admitted by those whom Strawson called the pessimists, for the ground of their pessimism is just this conviction that a belief in determinism provides us with a more fundamental reason than the usual reasons of insanity, ignorance, mistake, etc., for rejecting the moral participant attitudes. The pessimists may of course be wrong in thinking this. It may even turn out that this notion of a more fundamental reason cannot be made coherent. But in either case this will have to be made out. What cannot be assumed without begging the question is that there could not be a more fundamental reason of this sort. Yet this is just what Strawson seems to be assuming.

I must now turn to take a more direct look at the concept of desert. Strawson's British Academy lecture has been examined in some detail because he rightly sees the concept of desert as a tension point in the controversy between the pessimists and optimists. It is principally because the concept of desert seems to be edged out of the usual optimists' accounts of moral responsibility that the pessimists have *remained* pessimists . Strawson's aim was to show that the concept of desert finds its place in that "complicated web of attitudes and feelings which form an essential part of the moral life as we know it and which are quite opposed to objectivity of attitude."[9] If then, he argued, the complete repudiation of this web of attitudes and feelings is not even a live option for us, let alone demanded on rational grounds, the concept of desert remains unimpeached, regardless of the truth or falsity, coherence or incoherence, of the thesis of determinism. Now, though I have suggested that Strawson has failed in his attempt to show that the thesis of determinism (whatever it may be) is irrelevant to our moral reactive attitudes because his argument begs some fundamental questions, nevertheless I think he is essentially *right* in connecting the concept of desert with these attitudes and in suggesting that it is excluded from what he calls the 'objective attitude.' What his discussion fails to make clear is just why this is so. He is tantalizingly brief when it comes to telling us what the notion of desert is, hardly saying more than that we will see what it is if only "by attending to that complicated web of [interpersonal] attitudes and feelings."[10] What I want to do now, therefore, is (1) make more explicit why the notion of desert is to be found here and why it is excluded from the objective attitude; (2) show that Strawson was mistaken in thinking that an acceptance of the thesis of determinism is always irrelevant to the adoption of the objective attitude; (3)

show that to adopt the objective attitude is not necessarily to exclude all moral attitudes; and (4) suggest tentatively that the opposition between the optimists and pessimists is, in part, explicable by reference to individual differences of judgment as to what it is to be morally responsible and that these differences have their analogues in different sorts of moral temperament. I shall now deal with each of these points in turn.

(1) Why is Strawson right in suggesting that the notion of desert finds its place in the non-objective web of interpersonal relationships, and why is it so difficult to fit it into the 'objective attitude'? Primarily, I believe, because the notion of desert is conceptually linked with the notions of act and agent and it is these latter notions which are embedded in the participant attitudes and which tend to be excluded by the 'objective attitude'. Now the 'objective attitude' in Strawson's sense is characteristically that attitude we adopt toward a person when we see him perhaps "as an object of social policy; as a subject for what, in a wide range of sense, might be called treatment . . . to be managed or handled or cured or trained." We might add to this that it is the appropriate attitude to adopt if our aim is what might loosely be called 'scientific understanding', though this goes beyond what Strawson himself actually says. He is concerned to stress that it excludes the range of reactive feelings and attitudes which belong to involvement or participation with others in interpersonal relationships. It is equally important, I believe, to stress that the objective attitude includes looking for causal connections and forming and testing scientific hypotheses. Now, without at this point entering into a detailed discussion of the complex and related notions of act, agency, and intention, it is safe to say that it is notoriously difficult to fit these notions into a conceptual framework which purports to be in some sense scientific and objective. Anscombe, Hampshire, and Melden are only three of those who have helped us to see that this is so. The concept

of a human action is a social concept rather than a scientific one. It belongs to the interpersonal participant attitude rather than the objective. As A. I. Melden puts it, "Our concept of an action is the concept of an action for which the agent may have a reason and a reason of the kind that relates to the social intercourse of agents."[11] And again, "Where we are concerned with causal explanations, with events of which the happenings in question are effects in accordance with some law of causality, to that extent we are not concerned with human actions at all but, at best, with bodily movements or happenings."

Though I quote these passages from Melden with approval, I confess that the point that is being made has often been misunderstood and that elsewhere in his book Melden himself contributes to this misunderstanding. The point that I take from Melden is not that a reason for an action cannot in any sense be its cause. Indeed, Melden himself acknowledges that there is a perfectly familiar sense in which it is correct to speak of reasons as causes, a point not always given much publicity by Melden's critics. It is worth paying close attention to the following passage in which Melden expresses his aim: "The argument is designed to show the logical incoherence involved in the supposition that actions, desires, intentions, etc., stand in causal relations, either in the Humean sense or in any sense in which the term 'causal' is employed in the natural sciences."[13]

Though Donald Davidson is generally regarded as being in the opposite camp to Melden on the topic of reasons and causes, what Davidson says in his article 'Actions, Reasons, and Causes,'[14] far from being in opposition to the passage from Melden just quoted, seems to me to lend it considerable support. Admittedly, there is an ambiguity in Melden's reference to Humean causal relations which Davidson neatly exposes. To claim that A and B are causally related in a Humean sense may mean that there is some particular causal law linking A and B under those descriptions, or it may mean something weaker, namely, that there is a causal law, either known or discoverable, which is instantiated by *some* true descriptions of A and B though not necessarily by *any*. Davidson claims that it is only this second, weaker version of Hume's doctrine that can be made to fit with most causal explanations and that it fits equally well with explanations of actions in terms of reasons. Whether or not Melden would agree with this I do not know – nor does it matter, for the truth of the "weaker" version of Hume's doctrine is perfectly consistent with the point Melden was making in the passage quoted earlier. If this is so, it is understandable why. For, given that A is an event or state of affairs whose possible true description is given in terms of desires, intentions, wants, etc., and that B is an event or state of affairs whose true description is given in terms of human action, it could still be true both that A is the cause of B under *some* description of those terms, and that A and B can never be related by a Humean causal law when respectively described in terms of desires and actions. Not only does Davidson allow this as a theoretical possibility, but he seems to argue positively for the view that this is in fact what will necessarily be the case. In Davidson's own words: "The laws whose existence is required if reasons are causes of actions do not, we may be sure, deal in the concepts in which [reasons for actions] must deal. If the causes of a class of events (actions) fall in a certain class (reasons) and there is a law to back each singular causal statement, it does not follow that there is any law connecting events classified as reasons with events classified as actions – the classifications may even be neurological, chemical or physical."[15]

The proper moral to draw from all this, then, seems to be not that human behaviour is inexplicable in terms of causes nor even that it is not susceptible of scientific explanation, but rather that in any such explanation which was strictly scientific, the concept of human action would have no role to play. When, therefore, we adopt an attitude which is 'objective' in the sense in which it is usually tied to 'scientific', the related concepts of 'act', 'agent', and 'intention' all tend to slip through the net.

If this is so, it is understandable why the concept of desert slips through the net, too, because obviously this notion is inseparable from the concept of human action. Etymologically, the word "deserve" (according to the *Oxford English Dictionary*) is derived from the Latin "servire" meaning " to serve" together with the prefix "de" meaning "down to the bottom" and so "completely" or "thoroughly". Hence, one comes to 'deserve' something, in the central sense of having become worthy of reward or punishment, because one has well and truly *done* something. If then for any reason we adopt an attitude toward human bevaviour such that the conceptual framework appropriate to that attitude will more easily accommodate the notion of 'what-is-happening-to-people' than the notion of 'what-people-are-doing', then it should not surprise us that it will be difficult to accommodate in that framework the notion of desert.

(2) From what has just been said it should already be apparent why Strawson was mistaken in thinking that an acceptance of determinism is always irrelevant to the adoption of the objective attitude (with the consequent exclusion of the interpersonal participant attitudes). Whatever the thesis of determinism may be, it seems indisputable that those who accept it, or believe themselves to be accepting it, interpret its acceptance as being bound up with the adopting of the 'scientific attitude.' In fact, a case might be made out for the view that to accept the thesis of determinism is simply to adopt the scientific objective attitude toward all phenomena, including the phenomenon of human behaviour. But without pressing this point it is surely clear that, whatever the thesis of determinism may be, those who are convinced that its acceptance is in some sense rationally inescapable would

hardly want to deny its close association with the acceptance of the scientific attitude. The expression 'scientific determinism' is certainly as familiar to us as plain 'determinism,' even if it is no less obscure.

The point I want to stress is simply that, though the acceptance of 'scientific determinism' may well be rationally inescapable whenever it is our purpose to arrive at an objective scientific understanding of human behaviour, this is not always our purpose. Some human contexts, or rather, for the majority of us, most human contexts in which we find ourselves, call for the adoption of the participant interpersonal attitude toward human beings, and in these contexts the thesis of determinism (as Strawson in a way has shown us) just has no role to play. But it is highly misleading to suggest, as he does, that the acceptance of the thesis of determinism can have no implications for interpersonal attitudes because it clearly has, though not in the way that it is often thought to have. To adopt the thesis of determinism involves adopting a conceptual framework in which the notions associated with the participant attitudes (including the notion of desert) have no role to play, just as the adoption of the participant attitudes involves adopting a conceptual framework in which the concept of determinism has no role to play. But it would be absurd, of course, to imagine that we are faced with the choice of deciding which of these two attitudes is the more rational, as if we were required to commit ourselves permanently to one or the other. The rational thing to do is to adopt whichever attitude is appropriate to the particular context. It would be equally absurd to suppose that this called for a sort of schizophrenic frame of mind in which we neurotically vacillate from one attitude to the other. This would be to overlook that to say that a particular attitude is appropriate to the context is simply to say that it is suitable to our human purposes in that situation. Sometimes our purpose is to study another human being objectively and scientifically. Sometimes it is to be interpersonally involved with him. These purposes are different, but there can be no question of one being more legitimate than the other, nor of its being inconsistent to pursue both these ends. It is just that when we are doing one we are not doing the other.

Having made this contrast as clear as possible, I must now admit of course that the distinction is not nearly as sharp as I have drawn it. In practice it would doubtlessly be difficult, if not impossible, to find examples either of a purely objective attitude toward human behaviour or of a purely non-objective, participant attitude. I would not even like to try to give a detailed description of what such examples would be like if we were to come across them. Yet I am convinced that the contrast is real enough and that it represents, as it were, the opposite poles of an axis toward one or another of which most of the examples from real life would tend to cluster. All that need be claimed, then, is that the closer one moves to one pole of the axis, the more difficult it is to accommodate the concepts associated with the other. This need not prevent us from admitting that there is a continuum of examples from one pole to the other.

(3) It is this very mixture, usually in uneven proportions, of the participant and the objective attitudes which is given insufficient attention by Strawson insofar as he seems to think that the objective attitude excludes *all* moral attitudes. Though he himself denies that the contrasting attitudes are strictly exclusive of one another and claims that they *are* capable of being held to a greater or lesser degree, by selecting the participant attitude of resentment for particular attention and in rightly discerning it to be a *moral* attitude, he seems to have mistakenly concluded that *all* moral attitudes are of this interpersonal participant sort.

But there are also moral attitudes which find their proper place more toward the *objective* pole of the axis. In drawing the contrast between the participant and the objective attitudes, I have taken the latter to be most clearly typified in what I have loosely called the 'scientific attitude'. But we can be reasonably objective without going so far as being strictly scientific. I have already mentioned that Strawson thinks of the objective attitude as characteristically that attitude we adopt toward a person when we see him "as an object of social policy; as a subject for what, in a wide range of sense, might be called treatment . . . to be managed or handled or cured or trained."[16] What he overlooks is that there is a range of *moral* attitudes which are quite appropriate to this objective attitude. Cannot a social policy be morally good or bad? Are there not morally good and bad ways of managing, handling, curing, or training people? One does not have to be interpersonally involved with people in order to be morally and actively concerned for their good. It seems to me that, for example, much of the moral concern of the nineteenth century utilitarians for social reform, such as the treatment of prisoners, the sick, the insane, and the poverty-stricken, involved moral attitudes which find their expression nearer the objective than the participant pole of the axis. Where we go wrong is when we assume that these moral attitudes that find their expression in a relatively objective point of view exhaust the whole field of moral experience. This has tended to be the mistake of the utilitarians, most of whom have had strong sympathies with the scientific outlook and who have, therefore, found what may be called the objective-social moral attitudes the least difficult to accommodate to 'scientific-determinism'. For the same reason they have found it difficult to accommodate the participant moral attitudes basic to which is the concept of desert and which, as we have seen, is in turn conceptually linked with the notion of agency. Though, no doubt, all ethical theories have to make some use of the concept of human agency, I think there is little doubt that those theories in which it has a minimal role to play tend to be those whose authors have been convinced determinists. Their theories of punishment for example, have tended to be those where its justification is given exclusively in terms of its *effects* on the individual and society rather than by reference to what someone has *done*. It has been easier for them to see crime and immorality as a disease precisely because contracting a disease is something that *happens* to you, not something you *do*. And just as sometimes, though we are quite well, we are given an injection in order to *prevent* our getting a disease, so also some philosophers have not shrunk from the idea (or the ideal) of 'punishing' a man *before* he has committed a crime precisely in order to prevent him from committing it.

It is not necessarily, of course, a mistake to regard a person's behaviour in this objective way. It is only a mistake if we think it is the only possible way of so regarding it, or the only rational way. Whether it is the appropriate way or not will depend on the context of our particular purpose. If we are viewing the behaviour from a relatively objective, detached, 'scientific' point of view, then we will tend to describe, explain, and even morally evaluate a person's behaviour in a conceptual framework in which the concept of desert will have a minimum role to play. But if our purpose is to enter into some kind of interpersonal relationship with a human being (even if it is only to do this 'in imagination'), then the concept of desert will have a role to play, and an inescapable role at that, in our moral evaluation of the situation.

(4) This brings me to my last point where I make a few tentative and speculative suggestions which tie in with my opening remarks. I am aware that the argument I have been

putting forward grossly oversimplifies the situation and is in need of much more detailed qualification and filling out with concrete examples. Its aim has been to suggest a way of making the conflict between the pessimists and the optimists a little more intelligible and, therefore, presumably, more amenable to resolution. Strawson, I think, has already gone a long way toward doing this by showing the very important sense in which determinism is not destructive of our interpersonal moral attitudes. I have tried to go a little further by showing, first, the equally important sense in which it is destructive of them; second, that nevertheless determinism is not destructive of all our notions of morality; and third, that we are under no rational obligation to make some sort of permanent choice between the acceptance or rejection of determinism, for the rational justification of its acceptance or rejection (or rather its relevance or irrelevance) can only be given by reference to our ever-changing point of view ranging from the relatively interpersonal to the relatively objective.

My final and very tentative speculation is that, though in practice every individual's point of view will move up and down the scale according to the demand of varying circumstances, for some individuals the point of view adopted will tend to be nearer one pole, for others nearer the other. If, for example, by interest, training, and temperament, the 'scientific attitude' is the frame of mind which a person finds the more congenial, then it is perhaps inevitable that the notion of desert will appear somewhat suspect to his moral point of view. If, on the other hand, he happens to be one who by interest, training, and temperament is mostly concerned with the world of interpersonal relationships, then the notion of desert will play an essential role in his moral thinking, and the thesis of determinism will be suspect or else seen to be entirely irrelevant to practical life. I have tried to show that the mutual suspicions are unjustified, but no doubt a lot more attention will have to be paid to the varieties of moral goodness reflected in Tom, Dick, and Harry before such mutual suspicions can be finally allayed.

Notes

1. P. F. Strawson, 'Freedom and Resentment', *Proceedings of the British Academy* 48 (1962): 187–211.
2. J. H. Bernard, *The Works of Bishop Butler* (London: Macmillan, 1900), I:106f.
3. 'Freedom and Resentment', p. 192.
4. 'Freedom and Resentment', p. 194.
5. 'Freedom and Resentment'. The distinction between what he calls the 'participant attitude' and the 'objective attitude' has affinities with the distinction which Martin Buber drew between the 'I-thou relationship' and 'I-it' relationship (Martin Buber, *I and Thou*, trans. R. Gregor Smith [Edinburgh: T. & T. Clark, 1937]).
6. 'Freedom and Resentment', p. 195.
7. 'Freedom and Resentment', pp. 198–99.
8. 'Freedom and Resentment', p. 198.
9. 'Freedom and Resentment', p. 208.
10. Ibid.
11. A. I. Melden, *Free Action* (New York: Humanities Press, 1961), p. 196.
12. *Free Action*, p. 184.
13. *Free Action*, pp. 201–2.
14. Donald Davidson, 'Actions, Reasons, and Causes,' *Journal of Philosophy* 60, no. 23 (November 1963): 685–700.
15. 'Actions, Reasons, and Causes', p. 699.
16. 'Freedom and Resentment', p. 194.

Postscript

This paper was published in *Ethics* 79 (1969). I sent a copy to Professor Strawson, hoping for a critical comment, but received no reply.

4
The Alleged Limit to the Reach of Reason in Morality

Suppose there is a dispute between two or more parties concerning what is the case with respect to some matter of fact. Such a dispute can in principle be resolved rationally in so far as it is possible, in principle, to show which of the competing alternative beliefs a person would have the best reasons to accept. If a dispute arises concerning what is to be *done*, then this dispute can in principle be resolved rationally in so far it is possible, in principle, to show which of various alternative actions open to him a person would have the best reasons to do. (These remarks may be taken as reflecting the traditional distinction between theoretical reason and practical reason respectively.) We can now ask the following question: Are there any logical restrictions on how far disputes over what to do are capable in principle of being resolved rationally?

The frequent and tedious reiteration of the qualifying phrase "in principle" indicates that on the face of it my question doesn't concern human limitations, and has nothing to do with psychology. I am not asking how far human beings may be regarded as rational animals, but whether there are any logical restrictions on the scope of practical reason. Another point that needs to be made clear at this stage is that I am not concerned with what logical limits there may be to the scope of *theoretical reason*. There is an important sense in which factual questions concerning how things stand are logically prior to practical questions, and therefore whatever logical limitations there may be, if any, on the extent to which factual disputes may be resolved rationally, those same limitations would apply, a fortiori, to the rational resolution of practical disputes. But are there any *further* restrictions to the scope of practical reason *over and above* those which may belong to it by virtue of its involving theoretical reason? Can we know a priori that there are at least some species of practical disputes which are beyond the reach of reason in a sense in which disputes over questions of empirical fact are not?

I want now to sketch one case for the view that the arm of practical reason does indeed have a shorter reach than that of theoretical reason. Associated with this argument is a certain kind of theory of reasons for action. Essentially but crudely, it claims that what there is good reason for an agent to do will depend partly on what that agent's wants, needs or interests happen to be, and partly on what that agent has good reason to believe concerning certain matters of fact which relate to how his actions will be a means to satisfying or furthering his ends. Practical disputes therefore arise either through a clash of ends as reflected in a person's wants, needs or interests, or through clashes in the factual beliefs concerning means to ends, or, of course, in both these ways. The factual element in the dispute is the responsibility of theoretical reason, but clashes of wants, needs and interests are resolvable per media of social institutions, foremost of which is morality. The function of morality is to harmonise the satisfying of wants, needs and interests by providing social norms or principles which it is in the long-term common interests of all to regard as providing overriding reasons for action.

Clearly, to the extent that all parties to potential practical disputes recognise the existence of mutually agreed upon overriding reasons for action, there would be no theoretical difficulty in resolving such disputes rationally. However, according to the view I am expounding, there are several ways in which theoretical deadlock can often arise. By "theoretical deadlock" is meant a situation in which a disagreement (say between A and B) over what to do is not even *in principle* open to rational resolution. In such cases neither A's nor B's view can appropriately be described as irrational. There is no way in which it is even logically possible for reason to decide beween them. Instances of theoretical deadlock are generally thought to arise principally in one of the following three ways:

(1) The first may be described as deadlock between two committed moralists, each of whom regards moral principles as providing overriding reasons for action. This is the case, widely assumed to be quite common, where deadlock is traced to differences in so-called basic moral principles. Where such differences exist, provided neither party can be accused of holding inconsistent moral principles, or of acting inconsistently with them, reason is powerless to decide between them. So it is sometimes argued.

(2) The second type of deadlock is where a dispute arises between what we might call a committed moralist and a half-committed moralist. In this situation B may agree with A that it would be morally wrong for B to do x, and acknowledge that this provides a reason for his not doing x, but deny that it provides an *overriding* reason. B claims that other factors (maybe aesthetic or political considerations) provide weightier reasons *in favour* of his doing x. Again, it is alleged, where practical disputes are traceable to differences of this kind, theoretical deadlock is reached.

(3) A third type of theoretical deadlock arises between the committed moralist and the nihilist. In this situation, one party to the dispute may be quite indifferent to all moral considerations. He may well of course take into account the fact that other people allow moral considerations to influence their practical decisions, but he will do this only so far as it is necessary for furthering his own interests. For him, morality will be just one more sociological fact which, like any other

relevant fact, may have a bearing on what decisions he makes, but of itself will not provide him with any reasons for action whatever.

These are three ways (according to this theory) in which the scope of practical reason can be limited. In each of these three types of situation, there is no way, even in principle, of providing a rational solution to the disagreement. Again, so it has been argued.

One way of challenging this theory, popular among some philosophers, is to attack the theory of reasons-for-action which constitutes its foundation. However, I want to challenge it on its own ground, for with some qualifications I accept the view that reasons-for-action *are* grounded in wants or interests; but deny that such a theory of action has the implications for theoretical deadlock just outlined. In particular I want to show that there is no reason to believe that the arm of practical reason is shortened in any of the three situations. I am not going to argue that there are *no* logical limits to the reach of reason in the sphere of practical disputes, but simply that there is no good reason to believe that *if* there are any, they are any greater, or any different, from these which may be involved in the rational resolution of any dispute concerning questions of fact.

I must now no longer postpone saying something about theories of reasons-for-action which explicate such reasons in terms of wants, needs or interests. Anyone acquainted with some of the literature on the philosophy of action, (including David Richards's *A Theory of Reasons for Action*) will know that one has about the same chance of saying anything illuminating about reasons-for-action whether one expresses oneself briefly or at inordinate length. Encouraged by this thought let me say simply that for there to be a reason for an agent A to do an action x, it will have to be true that A's doing x is in some way in accordance with his wants or needs or interests. I deliberately express these three terms disjunctively because I suspect that no adequate theory of reasons for action can be made out in terms of any one, and yet it's certainly true that for there to be a reason for A to do x, A's doing x will have to be conducive to A's wants or needs or interests. The disjunctive expression is more cautious but also of course more vague and less illuminating. If any one of these three is more fundamental than the other two I suspect it is wants, but the concept of wanting is a labyrinth from which no one has yet managed to find a way through to the light. In the meanwhile we must be content with something a little less tidy.

It's important to notice that the possibility of alleged theoretical deadlock will be a challenge to any theory which claims for morality anything more than a severely limited rationality, and not just to a moral theory associated with a WNI (wants-or-needs-or-interests) theory of action. Nevertheless it certainly does present a challenge to this theory and the way it does I shall now try to make clear. According to the WNI view, there will be a reason for A to do an action x only if his doing that action is connected in some way with A's wants or needs or interests, no matter what that action x may be. Now it may be objected that this is just false, for couldn't it be true that A ought to do x regardless of A's wants or needs or interests? Now though the meaning of "A ought to do x" will vary with context, in general the force of this expression is simply to indicate that there is good reason for A to do x, without however indicating what that reason is. One who accepts a WNI theory of action is apparently therefore committed to the view that unless A's doing x is in some way in accordance with A's wants or needs or interests it can't be true that x is something which A ought to do. Can this view be defended?

One well-worn line of defence is to argue that in the long run one's moral duty and interests always coincide. Though valiant and ingenious attempts have been made to show this, none of them in my view succeed. I think that we have to accept that on occasions doing what is right or just may involve sacrificing even one's long-term interests. Nevertheless, there will still be a reason for A to do his duty even in situations of this kind if A wants to do that very action which would mean the sacrifice of his own long-term interests. Of course he will not want to do x *under that description*, but perhaps under the description "that action which will save my friend's life" or even "that action which I see to be my duty". It is of the first importance to notice that acceptance of a wants theory of action doesn't commit the holder to some form of egoism. Incidentally, this is one reason in favour of regarding wants rather than interests as being more fundamental in providing reasons for action. What is in a person's interests seems too closely tied to what will profit him, or what will be to his gain, for any theory of reasons for action based on this concept alone to give a non-paradoxical account of disinterested or altruistic action. But that a person should want to sacrifice their life rather than betray their friend isn't paradoxical at all, for such a person doesn't of course want to sacrifice their life. What they want in preference to saving their own life, if this involves betraying their friend, is being faithful to their friend, even if this involves losing their own life. But to prefer the latter alternative is hardly in their interests.

However, though a holder of a WNI theory can explain how altruistic actions are possible, it's clear that the main challenge has not yet been met. For according to this theory, moral convictions will provide reasons for action only because such convictions mediate the fundamental, long-term preferences or wants of the agents holding them. In so far therefore as two parties to a practical dispute find themselves in disagreement over what they take to be basic moral principles, they will apparently have irreconcilable opinions on what there is good reason to do simply because the satisfying of their basic wants or preferences will be incompatible. The alleged deadlock between the committed moralist and the half-committed moralist, or between the moralist and the nihilist will be similarly traceable to a disharmony between what is sometimes called their "ultimate reasons for action". Given that the parties to the dispute are not ignorant of any relevant matters of fact, how can such deadlocks be resolved? How can there be any more work for reason to do?

I think there is plenty more work for reason to do, but before going on to say why, I would like to consider an important possible objection to the WNI theory of action as I have presented it. It might plausibly be argued that though indeed it is not possible to make sense of a reason for action which is unconnected with *anyone's* wants or interests, the connection is somewhat different from what I have suggested. It might be said that for there to be a reason for A to do x, it won't be necessary that A's doing x is in some way connected with A's wants or interests. For, if A's doing x is in the general interests of the community at large, then this of itself is a reason for A to do x, even though of course it won't provide A with a reason for doing it. Now in so far as the very point of morality is to protect and further the interests of the community as a whole, then whether or not A has a reason for doing x it could still be true that there is reason for A to do x, and this could in principle be objectively demonstrated by showing that A's doing x was in the best interests of the community as a whole. Thus, the rationality and objectivity of morality is in no way impugned by the fact that it is not always possible to move a person to do what there is nevertheless good reason for them to do.

I have described this argument as plausible, for it appears to combine the virtues of a theory of action with a satisfying notion of rational objectivity. However, the appearance of objectivity is illusory. Though it is certainly important to distinguish between "A has a reason to do x" and "There is a reason for A to do x", it is equally important to notice that the latter expresses a value judgment whereas the former does not. If someone says "There is a reason for A to do x" then the person making that claim is indicating that A's doing x is in accordance with the *speaker's* wants or needs or interests. It may be that what the speaker wants is that A's action should protect or serve the interests of the general community. Only in so far as this want is shared however can there be rational agreement for the claim "There is reason for A to do x". And of course this want may not be shared, and in particular it may not be shared by A. However, though the marking of the distinction between "A has reason to do x" and "There is reason for A to do x" won't of itself show that reason can break the deadlock, it does point to an important modification that we need to make to an alleged implication of wants theories of action. I said earlier that anyone who accepts a wants theory of action is apparently committed to the view that unless A's doing x is in some way in accordance with A's wants or interests it can't be true that x is something which A ought to do. It is now clear that this implication is indeed apparent only. If I claim that A ought to do x I am not necessarily implying that A's doing x is in accordance with A's wants or interests but I am implying that it is in accordance with mine. Not necessarily my *interests* of course but in some sense my wants, for unless I judge A's doing x together with whatever consequences I foresee will follow from this as something which I would want in preference to any alternative action (together with its consequences) which I see as a reasonable option for A, then it would be false for me to say that there is good reason for A to do x, or in other words, "A ought to do x".

All this might seem to some to make morality incurably subjective and to underline even more firmly the impression that wants theories of action point to the inevitability of the deadlock we mentioned earlier. How can there be any more work for reason to do once we trace fundamental disagreements over what there is reason to do to fundamental incompatibilities between the basic wants and preferences of the individuals concerned?

The only way to answer this question is to make a nervous and tentative excursion into that labyrinth called the concept of wanting. Perhaps the most fundamental blunder in connection with wants is to think of them as essentially involving some sort of inner psychological disturbance. When therefore we trace differences of opinion concerning what ought to be done, to differences in fundamental wants, we are apt to think that we have traced the difference back to brute psychological facts which we think of as the person's "ultimate" reasons for action. However, what needs to be said clearly is that inner psychological disturbances are not reasons for action at all, let alone ultimate reasons. Wants which are reasons for action are a species of belief. To want x is to believe that one would enjoy x, or believe that x is a state of affairs which one would welcome or prefer to any foreseen alternative; or, of course, to want x may be to believe that x is a means to any of these. Furthermore not only are wants which are reasons for action a species of belief, but also the beliefs involved normally, perhaps always, go beyond one's own present or future state of mind. Wants are beliefs which reach out into the world. Particularly is this true of wants which we might describe as long-term or fundamental. Beliefs about the world are corrigible. Therefore wants which constitute reasons for action are peculiarly suitable targets for rational criticism. Far from being the case then that tracing practical disputes to differences in fundamental wants constitutes reaching the point beyond which reason cannot go, the work which remains for reason to do would seem to extend indefinitely.

One thing which has made it difficult to appreciate the corrigible nature of wants is the fact that although there is an important sense in which individuals are the authorities on what they want, like other authorities they can be mistaken.

As Hampshire has shown, to claim that one wants x is in an important sense to have made a decision of which one is necessarily the author. But decisions can be revised or revoked in the light of further evidence. In so far as wants are beliefs, and beliefs which are at least in part about the world outside of one's own mental states, then the possibility is always open for these wants to be changed or modified as a result of coming to see the objects of one's wants in new ways, or under aspects hitherto unnoticed. The bringing about of such changes and modifications is at least as much a function of rational discussion as the searching out of inconsistencies and the tracing of logical implications. Once this is appreciated, one can see the fallacy in the claim that if two parties to a practical dispute are agreed on all the relevant facts then if their ultimate reasons for action are incompatible the reach of reason has found its limit. There are two fundamental roots to the fallacy.

Firstly, to claim that two parties are agreed on all the relevant facts can only mean that neither has made any factual claim which the other has regarded as both relevant and false. What it cannot mean is that their examination of the relevant facts has been exhaustive, for, of course, there are an infinite number of such facts. Secondly, the claim pictures a ludicrously crude distinction between facts about means to ends and what might be called psychological facts about an individual's inner springs of action. This model for an understanding of reasons for action is almost totally wrong, for the wants that constitute reasons for action are thoroughly thought-dependent and thought-impregnated. They are more appropriately described as beliefs than as psychological urges, and of course thoughts and beliefs are all grist to reason's mill.

We are now I believe in a position to see just how misleading all talk of "ultimate reasons" and "ultimate wants" can be. Ironically, Richard Norman in *Reasons for Action* attacks all theories which base reasons for action on wants principally because he sees all such theories as being committed to the notion of ultimate reasons for action – "ultimate" in the sense of being unquestionable, incorrigble, and constituted by first-person psychological statements. However, no such implication is involved. Though it may be true that reasons for action must ultimately make reference to wants, it doesn't follow from this either that there are 'ultimate wants' or that there are ultimate reasons for action in the required sense. The Humean point that all series of questions which ask for reasons for action must stop at some point doesn't entail that there is some point at which all such series of demands must stop. Sometimes, the ultimate answer to the qustion "Why did you do that?" might be "Because that was my moral duty". Depending on the context, to respond with "How do you know?" could well be inappropriate. This is not to admit that the agent's reason for action is beyond the reach of rational criticism, nor that nothing could be said by the agent by way of giving it rational support. When I once claimed in a class discussion (as I thought innocuously) that it was wrong to torture children, someone remarked "How do you know?". My reaction was to regard the question as simply inappropriate, but this is not because my judgment that the immorality of torturing children is so basic or rockbottom as to be beyond the possibility of rational support. Rather, assuming the question to be sincere, I didn't quite know what the questioner was getting at. Did he doubt it? Did he think it's arguable whether it's wrong? What possible objection to my claim did he have in mind? All this is not to suggest that it is in some sense self-evident, or impossible for anyone but a madman to deny. Sane men have denied it. It is simply that until rather more is known of what is in the questioner's mind, and in particular how he views children and the infliction of pain, what things he enjoys and what things he shuns; until some of these things are known one cannot know where to begin. But once some of these things *are* known, the scope of rational criticism of his views, *and* mine extends indefinitely.

Linked with the thought-dependent nature of wants which provide reasons for action is another feature of wants which also has an obvious connection with their being suitable objects of rational criticism, namely their hierarchical nature. We may want x, but may want y, which is incompatible with x, even more. Many of the things we want are such that for us to have them all would be logically impossible. We can want something under one description, and not want it under another equally true description, such as when a man wants to be both married and single. It is this feature of wants which allows us to say both that someone can have good reason to do x even if he doesn't want to do it, and that unless he wants to do x he cannot have good reason to do it. The paradox disappears given different but equally true descriptions of the same referent x.

In short, wants are things that we order, reflect upon, justify, criticise, discover, make up our minds about, identify, and misidentify. Moreover, because they have these features they are essentially modifiable by the activity which we call rational criticism and enquiry – essentially because the connection between modifying thoughts and modifying wants is not contingent but analytic.

To conclude I would like to make it clear both what I have aimed to do and what I have not aimed to do. It has been no part of my purpose to try to show that we can be hopeful and optimistic about people resolving moral differences in a rational manner. I have not tried to demonstrate that *homo sapiens* is an essentially rational being and that, given a little encouragement, fundamental disputes between people on moral issues will all eventually dissolve in the acids of rational criticism. Nor do I think that my argument gives the slightest support to this view, for I have not been concerned at all with the practical limitations imposed upon any attempt to resolve moral disagreements rationally – limitations that arise from such factors as prejudice, ignorance, pigheadedness, vanity, lack of intelligence and just plain wickedness. These factors appear to be formidable barriers indeed, and I'm afraid I tend to be rather pessimistic in my expectations concerning whether human beings will have the capacity to resolve their most serious practical problems in a rational manner. What I have been concerned to show is that, though the practical barriers to the rational resolution of such problems may indeed be immense, perhaps even insuperable, there is no reason to believe that there are any logical limits to the scope of reason in the sphere of the moral, or if there are, that they are any greater, or essentially any different, from those that apply in the sphere of empirical fact. If the argument is sound (or even if it's not, but its conclusion is true) there is perhaps one practical implication which may be worth noting. Insofar as people abandon the conviction that the deep-rooted differences on moral questions which divide them, and which divide nations, are fundamentally due to some sort of intrinsic limit in the sphere of the moral, then perhaps their efforts to overcome the practical barriers of prejudice, etc. will be a little more vigorous and determined than they would otherwise be; for no sane person will put their heart into a project which they believe is logically impossible to pull off. But this practical consequence (if indeed it should turn out to be such) would be a bonus. I shall be more than content if what I have said in this paper is even roughly true.

Note

This paper is a revised version of a paper titled 'Wants, beliefs and reasons' which I read at the NZ Philosophy Conference at Waikato University in 1973.

5
Reason, Faith and Freedom

I begin with a quotation:

> Only when we ourselves *voluntarily* recognise God, desiring to enter into relationship with him, can our knowledge of him be compatible with our freedom, and so with our existence as personal beings. If God were to reveal himself to us in the coercive way in which the physical world is disclosed to us, he would thereby annihilate us as free and responsible persons. (J. Hick, *Faith and Knowledge*, p. 134).

This quotation comes from the chapter entitled 'Faith and Freedom' in Hick's book and expresses its central point. His argument in that chapter is itself representative of an argument widely used in Christian theology – perhaps more particularly in liberal Protestant theology (though, as we shall see later, it also has some support from Catholic writers).

In broad outline, the argument goes like this:

(1) Belief in God's existence is not something which is susceptible of rational demonstration or 'proof'. (This is a typically 'protestant' view.)

(2) Nevertheless, religious belief can be 'reasonable'. (This is the liberal/protestant emphasis.) The facts of history, our experience of the world about us, but especially moral experience and what is broadly termed 'religious' experience, both corporal and individual – all this provides the proper basis for a Christian believer to claim that his faith has some sort of 'rational foundation', or is in some sense consistent with his being a reasonable creature. The advocate of this

argument denies that Christian belief is contrary to all reason, or that becoming a Christian involves sacrificing one's rationality.

(3) The 'evidence' appealed to is admitted however to be open to other interpretations. It will appear convincing only to the eye of faith. In itself it will always remain ambiguous. When Christians are asked to give a reason for the hope that is in them, they will always be able to point to relevant considerations – acts and experiences which for them point to the truth of what they believe, but which they will admit may to others be not unreasonably open to some secular or naturalistic interpretation. Because of this radical ambiguity of the evidence when viewed from any objective standpoint (if that were indeed possible) there can never be any question of proof or demonstration.

(4) But this itself is reasonable, and is only to be expected, in view of the nature of the God believed in. God is a God of love who therefore cannot (without acting contrary to his own nature) force himself upon men. He respects our dignity as free, responsible agents which we have by virtue of being his creation, and seeks to awaken in us a free loving response to his own love. Hence, all of us have the opportunity of accepting or rejecting, believing or disbelieving, of our own free will. There can be no question of being compelled to believe.

(5) Hence (a) Both the wickedness and futility of all attempts to compel belief at the point of the sword. It doesn't make sense to force persons 'freely' to respond to God's love, which is what they seek. (b) This explains why arguments between believers and non-believers are always inconclusive, and particularly why it is absurd to attempt to convince anyone of the truth of Christian claims by rational argument – for if this were possible, then provided they had a clear head and the capacity to follow the argument where it leads, they would have no option but to believe, and this would mean violating

their freedom no less seriously than if they were forced to believe at the point of a sword.

The argument just outlined I hope will be recognised as central in a great deal of Protestant theology, more particularly perhaps of this century but certainly not confined to it. John Hick, whose own form of the argument I have largely followed (though with some variations and embellishments which however I would not expect him to object to) has claimed that the principle at issue has long been recognised, and among those who saw it clearly he mentions Samuel Taylor Coleridge, Pascal, Hugh of St Victor and Irenaeus. It is the doctrine of veiled revelation, the belief in a deus absconditus, who, in the words of Hugh of St Victor, "from the beginning wished neither to be entirely manifest to human consciousness nor entirely hidden." In Coleridge's words, the divine existence "could not be intellectually more evident without becoming morally less effective, without counteracting its own end by sacrificing the life of faith to the cold mechanism of a worthless because compulsory assent."

The argument raises, as I hope to show, some issues of philosophical importance which range beyond the philosophy of religion – issues which are in fact very complex and certainly very difficult to deal with satisfactorily in a single paper. Nevertheless, I propose to give some kind of sketch of them which will I hope be sufficient to indicate that the argument under discussion, if not fundamentally fallacious, is certainly far too frail a structure to support the weight it has been called upon to bear. If it is to continue to be pressed into service, it is in urgent need of strengthening and renovation.

In particular, two related philosophical issues of central importance are involved, and I shall be discussing them in conjunction with each other. They are:

> (1) To what extent and in what ways is belief in general, and religious belief in particular, a matter of the will?

(2) In what sense do argument, reasons, evidence, experience 'compel' belief, and how is such compulsion and its implied restriction of freedom related to our freedom and integrity as responsible agents with a capacity for entering into personal relationships?

These are big questions. I propose to do no more than suggest that a preliminary investigation of them points to answers which are almost wholly destructive of the argument under consideration, and that if that argument therefore is to be continued to be employed, the prima facie difficulties which these questions raise will have to be shown to be prima facie only.

Firstly, however, it is important not to overlook a point of central importance to the argument, which is I believe obviously true, viz. that it is absurd to speak of forcing someone to respond in love and trust. You can force someone to sham love, to pretend but not genuinely to love. Similarly with trust. Love and trust can be evoked but not 'compelled' or 'demanded', or if they can it is only in the sense that love compels and demands, and not in the sense that the tyrant does. To speak of being constrained by love is not to complain of a lack of freedom. When the Christian sings

Love so amazing, so divine
Demands my soul, my life, my all

he is singing a song of liberty. The paradox that to respond to love's demands is to find one's true freedom no doubt is a paradox which requires a little explaining, which however I don't intend to attempt now. For the purposes of this paper I simply record my conviction that it is a paradox, and not a self-contradiction, and that it enshrines an important truth. If God seeks a loving response from his creatures then he cannot force us to love him – and this, of course, is no real limitation of his power.

But the important question at issue is: Would God's unambiguous revelation of himself constitute a coercion of any kind? Why couldn't God unambiguously reveal the reality of his existence and still leave his creatures free either to reject him or to respond to him in loving obedience?

Hick's answer to this question is clear. He admits that belief in the reality of God can be distinguished in thought from a practical trust and obedience towards him, but adds that in fact they go together and depend closely on one another. (p. 144) To believe that God exists is to believe in the existence of an infinitely superior Creator on whom his creatures depend, and to whom they owe loving obedience. To come to recognise the excellence of such a being involves a complete reorientation of one's whole vision of life and order of values. In short, because there is no possibility of God's revealing his reality without at the same time revealing the implications of it for the lives of his creatures in terms of worship and loving obedience, any unambiguous revelation of himself would mean that the atheist (for example) would be forced to acknowledge that there is one to whom he owes loving obedience, and such a coercion would necessarily be a violation of his human freedom, and therefore would not after all bring about the spontaneous and free loving response which it is God's purpose to evoke. Baldly stated then, the essential points of the argument are as follows:

> (1) If God unambiguously revealed himself, or if his existence were demonstrable, then we would or could be forced to acknowledge his existence.
> (2) To acknowledge God's existence necessarily entails acknowledging certain far-reaching moral (or quasi-moral) claims, e.g. that we ought to love and obey him.
> (3) Acknowledging moral claims can't be forced upon us without doing violence to our integrity as free responsible human personalities. Therefore, God cannot unambiguously reveal himself, or allow his

existence to be demonstrable, without infringing our freedom.

One way of interpreting this argument would be to understand belief in God in Braithwaitean terms. Acceptance of the indemonstrability of God's existence would then be an instance of the acceptance of the general principle that ultimate moral principles can't be demonstrated but are in some important sense a matter of 'choice' or 'decision'. Hick makes it quite clear however that he rejects a Braithwaitean analysis of belief in God. For him, whether or not God exists is a matter of ontological fact and is certainly not dependent on anyone's choice or decision, either directly or indirectly. Nevertheless, according to Hick, if anyone acknowledges the ontological fact of God's existence he is thereby acknowledging some kind of moral commitment. It follows that, for Hick, coming to know of the fact of God's existence has got to be a matter of the will, something which we can freely accept or reject.

I want to argue that, for the purposes of this argument, it doesn't matter whether we interpret belief in God in Braithwaitean terms or not. For if it can be shown that being 'forced' to believe something by being faced with the relevant evidence, or by rational argument, can never involve a violation of a person's freedom (in the relevant sense of freedom), then it won't matter whether what we are 'forced' to believe in this way is some matter of ontological fact, or some sort of moral fact, or some sort of curious combination of the two.

Though it needs some qualification it seems true that belief is not a matter of the will. Believing is not something we are free to do, or not to do, for in an important sense it is not something we do at all. It is not an action or an activity. The most obvious way of showing that belief is not a matter of the will is to issue invitations to people to believe something. Try believing that last weekend I climbed to the top of Mt Everest. If it's replied that this is indeed difficult to believe, this might be thought to suggest that you might succeed if I offered something easier. Would you believe – Mt Cook? Mt Egmont then? But if I asked you to believe that last weekend I climbed Mt Egmont, and you did believe this, this wouldn't be because you complied with my request, or if you didn't believe it, that you refused my request. Rather it would be because my asking you to believe it – including the manner of my asking, my tone of voice, twinkle in my eye, etc. – constituted evidence for or against the claim, and depending on whether that evidence combined with other relevant evidence seemed to you either to support, or count against the claim, or neither, you either believed, disbelieved or simply formed no opinion one way or the other. Notice that if asking you to believe something showed that belief was a matter of the will then it would make sense to order you to believe something, or to forbid you to believe it. But there surely is something absurd about these locutions, though I'm not denying that in ordinary usage we sometimes come across them. No doubt people have from time to time been 'forbidden' to believe that the world moves, or that man shares a common ancestor with the ape, or that communism is preferable to capitalism, but if these expressions mean anything coherent at all they are not prohibitions against believing something but against expressing that belief, or entertaining the belief or attending to the relevant evidence. Indeed, in this latter sense belief can be said to be indirectly within our control because we can by various techniques, including some varieties of meditation, bring it about that we believe something when at the moment we either don't believe it or neither believe nor disbelieve it. We can take steps to expose ourselves to the evidence, or to part of the evidence, or protect ourselves from some or all of the evidence. Or we may voluntarily undergo some psychological or neuropsychological treatment which would alter our beliefs and disbeliefs. But this doesn't show that believing is a matter of the will: it merely shows that exposing ourselves to or protecting ourselves from the evidence, submitting to brainwashing or indoctrination, etc. is a matter of the will. The fact that we can take steps to bring it about that we believe something no more makes believing a matter of the will than does the fact that we can take steps to bring it about that we feel warm or feel happy make feeling warm or feeling happy a matter of the will.

It might be objected at this point that almost all of the examples of belief so far employed have been beliefs about empirical matters of fact. It might be admitted that we can't at will, in the face of contrary evidence, believe (say) that there are mushroom farms on the moon, or that Julius Caesar coughed at midday on the day following his sixth birthday. But the case is different with moral beliefs. These (it is sometimes alleged) are in some sense a matter of decision and "we are free to form our own moral opinions in a much stronger sense than we are free to form our own opinion as to what the facts are." The last part of this sentence will be recognised as a quotation from Hare's *Freedom and Reason* and it will be remembered that Hare believes that this freedom to form our own moral beliefs is a consequence of the doctrine that there can be no logical deduction of moral judgments from purely factual premisses.

My reply to this is that, whether or not that doctrine is true, it is irrelevant to the point at issue. For if moral beliefs were a matter of the will, then it would make sense to order someone to accept or reject some moral belief. There admittedly might be moral objections to doing this, but these would not be logical objections to it. But of course there are logical objections to it, for it no more makes sense to order someone to believe that apartheid is morally wrong than to order them to believe that fluoridation of the water supply is dentally beneficial. It may well be that our considered moral opinions are some sort of product of our factual beliefs and some of our fundamental long term desires or wants. But it is even more difficult to see how the latter could be something that was under the control of the will, for the concept of the will itself, and the connected concepts of choice and decision, presuppose wants and desires. No doubt, as with beliefs, one can bring it about that some at least of our wants and desires are changed but this is presumably because more fundamental wants and desires form the springs of action necessary to bring about these changes. I am not suggesting that our fundamental wants and desires never change, or that they can't be modified by suitable techniques, including (perhaps) by the possessor of those wants and desires being exposed to rational argument. What I am suggesting is that if it is proper to speak at all of fundamental wants and desires, then it is far from clear how they could be altered or modified at will. Hence, in so far as moral beliefs are in part a product of fundamental wants and desires, they are no more obviously under the control of the will than our beliefs about matters of fact.

If then neither factual nor moral beliefs are a matter of the will, it is clear that if we speak of being 'forced' to believe something by evidence, then this sense of 'forced' is quite harmless and can in no way constitute a restriction of our freedom in the sense in which a restriction of our freedom is some sort of deprivation of human liberty. We could only be 'forced' in this vicious sense if belief was normally a matter of the will – something we either choose to do or to refrain from doing. But if, as I have argued, belief is not a matter of the will, then evidence or argument cannot possibly force us to believe something *against* our will any more than it can assist us to believe something *in accordance with* our will.

It is important to notice that I am not denying that some things we believe we wish were not so, or that some things we disbelieve we wish were so. Nor am I denying that it is possible for people to come to believe something precisely because they want it to be true. Nor, of course, am I denying that people can come to hold irrational beliefs, unsupported by any relevant evidence, or even beliefs which are incompatible with all the relevant evidence. There are in fact numerous ways, some of which I have referred to, in which we can bring it about that beliefs, both our own and others', can be modified, altered, created, destroyed. Some of these ways of modifying other people's beliefs do indeed involve a restriction on their freedom and some sort of violation of their nature as free, responsible human beings but, far from it being the case that presenting people with the relevant evidence restricts their freedom, in general (as I shall show later) this is the only way of modifying the beliefs of others which does not restrict their freedom.

To make it quite clear why evidence can't constitute a restriction of freedom in any morally relevant sense let us take an example. Suppose that q is in fact conclusive evidence for p. Then if we present A (who, up till now, doesn't believe p) with the evidence q, and A sees that q is conclusive evidence for p, then if A is rational A now does believe p. This presentation of the evidence for p could only mean a restriction of A's freedom in any significant sense if it were possible for A either to believe p or to believe not-p independently of either seeing p as true or seeing p as false. But to believe p is to see p as true, and to believe not-p is to see p as false. If A then changes from seeing p as false to seeing p as true as a result of being faced with the relevant evidence, this can't be a restriction on A's freedom, for what was A free to do before which A is no longer free to do now? If it is replied that A is now no longer free to see p as false, then I answer that this is no loss of freedom, for even in this sense of freedom, when A saw p as false before being presented with the evidence q, A wasn't free to see p as true. Moreover, if A neither believed nor disbelieved p before being presented with the evidence q, then again the fact that A now sees p as true is no loss of freedom, for before being presented with the evidence A wasn't free to see p as true or to see p as false. Being confronted with relevant evidence for or against a belief cannot possibly therefore constitute a diminution or overriding of freedom in any sense of 'freedom' which is connected with our status as morally responsible human beings.

Now it's only fair to point out that Hick himself has conceded that the sense in which experience or evidence is coercive of belief is irrelevant to our freedom as morally responsible agents. Or rather, he has conceded that this is so as far as our experience of the physical world is concerned. He thinks the case is different, however, when we consider religious experience. In reply to Duff-Forbes who has also objected to the notion that evidence and argument are destructive of our freedom, Hick has offered a defence whose substance amounts to the following: he agrees that to be 'forced' to have certain beliefs about the physical world on the basis of our experience doesn't constitute a restriction of our freedom in any morally relevant sense. However, he argues that were our experience of the supernatural world to compel us to believe some things about it, and not others, the compulsion involved would constitute a violation of our freedom as autonomous moral agents. Hick claims that all conscious experience, whether of the natural or the supernatural, is "experience-as", and by this he means that all experience involves an element of interpretation. In the case of our experience of the physical world, our interpretation of that experience is forced upon us by what he calls rewards and penalties – rewards for interpreting correctly and penalties for interpreting incorrectly. However, with regard to our experience of God and the world of supernature, because such a world is what he calls "value laden", there could be no immediate rewards and penalties for correct and incorrect interpretations, for this would involve an overriding of our moral freedom. The supernatural always presents itself to us in a manner which leaves us free to interpret our experiences if we will in purely naturalistic terms. When God presents himself to us he does so in a manner which leaves us entirely free to regard such an experience as not an experience of God at all but as some purely naturalistic phenomenon. Faith is the interpretive element in our experience of the supernatural. Those who have faith will experience certain events in their lives and in the lives of others as manifestations of God's presence, his love and his power, whereas those who are without it will experience the same events as having no more than naturalistic significance. Which interpretation we adopt must be entirely up to us. Our becoming aware of God must be a free and uncompelled response to his love. (Hick makes a number of other points in his reply to Duff-Forbes some of which he might regard as essential to his argument, but which for lack of time I must ignore.)

In my judgment his fundamental mistake is that he appears to regard believing as some sort of activity. This enables him to speak as if we had conscious motives for belief, for only if believing is some sort of action or activity will it be appropriate to speak of motives for belief. That he does regard this as appropriate is I think clear from my summary of his argument. He assumes that reasons for believing are like reasons for action at least in this respect, that they are connected with wants and desires. All experience in his view involves interpretation and this interpretation he explicitly speaks of as an "activity". Moreover, he speaks of "interpreting" as something which can be done "correctly" or "incorrectly", and it's clear that he means that one who interprets correctly believes truly and one who interprets incorrectly believes falsely. Hence, he can say "there are immediate rewards for interpreting correctly and immediate penalties for interpreting incorrectly in relation to the physical world but not in relation to God". It seems clear then that when Hick speaks of evidence and experience as "compelling" belief, the kind of compulsion he has in mind is that which would be provided by strong prudential considerations. Hence his insistence that while such compulsion is operative concerning our beliefs about the physical world, it is as it were quite innocuous, but with value-laden 'religious' experiences our interpretations must be strictly uncompelled if our moral freedom is to be respected.

The confusion at the centre of Hick's position is his regarding believing as a kind of conscious activity, and hence when he thinks of our being compelled to believe something by arguments, evidence, and experience, he thinks of the 'compulsion' as being of a piece with the compulsion we experience when forced to hand over our wallet at gunpoint. But as I have already argued, we have here utterly different kinds of compulsion. When I am compelled by the evidence, there are no restrictions of any kind placed on what I can do, for believing isn't something that I 'do', and therefore not something that I do either freely or unfreely.

But of course we do speak of 'freedom of belief', and there is a genuine and important sense in which freedom to believe is something to be valued and cherished, and the depriving of which does constitute a violation of the integrity of the human personality. I hope we are now in a better position to see just what that freedom is. Genuine freedom of belief, far from being the freedom to form our opinions independently of the relevant evidence is, on the contrary, the freedom to form our opinions unhampered and unfettered by anything other than the relevant evidence. It is the opportunity to form our opinions free of all the influences of propaganda, indoctrination, high-pressure advertising, drugs, brainwashing, etc. – in short all causal agencies which seek to mould opinion in any way other than by the impartial and objective presentation of all the relevant evidence, both for and against. Connected with this idea is the notion of being free to express beliefs without fear of persecution or hostile social disapproval, or political threats and the like. It is factors of these sorts which constitute a real threat to freedom of belief, and it's to be noticed that none of these restrictions presuppose that belief itself is a matter of the will. What is a matter of the will is the examining of reasons, the assembling of arguments, the paying attention to evidence, the balancing of pros and cons. It is these activities whose restriction constitutes a lack of freedom to believe. The one thing that does not and cannot constitute a restriction of freedom to believe is evidence itself.

My conclusion then is that the argument which sets out to show that the evidence for the existence of a God of love must necessarily be ambiguous, for were it anything else this would constitute an infringement of our freedom, an infringement which a God of love could not allow without being inconsistent with his nature, is not only a seriously fallacious argument but also backfires rather badly. For it would seem that far from unambiguous evidence constituting a threat to our freedom and an overriding of our nature as responsible beings, it is only when evidence alone is allowed to determine our belief that we have genuine freedom of belief. It is the deliberate withholding of such evidence therefore, rather than the supplying of it, which would seem to constitute the real violation of our personal freedom.

One final point. The essential things that I have said about the relevance of evidence to belief will I think apply to both "belief that" and "belief in", when the latter expression is construed as being roughly equivalent to "trust in". In so far as trust in x presupposes belief that x exists then, in so far as the evidence points against the existence of x, to that extent trust in x would be shown to be misplaced. Moreover, even when the existence of x is not in doubt, though trust necessarily always reaches beyond the evidence, it is always founded on some evidence that the one in whom trust is placed is indeed trustworthy. My concern here is simply to point out that trustees don't in any way threaten the liberty or override the personality of trusters by furnishing them with additional evidence about themselves. Trust is made necessary by having less than conclusive evidence, but in a world in which nothing was hidden, trust would be unnecessary. Will we avoid getting to know too much about our friends in order to make it possible for us to continue to trust them? And what would we think of friends who deliberately kept both the question of their existence and the nature of their character ambiguous in order to respect the freedom of those whom they loved? If we didn't regard them as morally perverse we would think them just plain crazy.

A final postscript. The argument designed to justify the hiddenness of God and the ambiguity of the evidence for his existence *seems* radically inconsistent wlth the central theme of Christian eschatology, which is that, in the end, God's existence will be made plain to all. However, whether or not eschatological theology concedes all the points I have argued for would provide material for another paper.

Postscript

This paper was originally a contribution to a Religious Studies Colloquium held at the University of Auckland in August, 1974. lt subsequently appeared in *Perspectives on Religion: NZ Viewpoints 1974*, edited by John C. Hinchcliff and published by the University of Auckland Bindery in 1975.

My principal reason for offering this paper to the Colloquium was that I once accepted the view that to be 'forced' to accept a belief by means of a convincing rational argument was in some sense an infringement of one's freedom as an autonomous rational agent. I wanted to show that this is in fact a serious mistake, arising from regarding belief as an action or activity directly under the control of the will. The implications for the common assumption that we should be free to believe whatever we like, as opposed to the freedom to express our beliefs, should now be clearer.

6
Human Rights

A paper read at a conference on *Human Rights and Foreign Policy* in Dunedin, May 1976

No one is surprised when early in any discussion on the topic of sport, politics or international affairs there is talk of people's rights, and later, as the argument begins to call forth the higher flights of rhetoric, of *human* rights. Are these expressions nothing more than emotional props which orators use when the logic of their arguments begins to sag, or do they point to an important factor in the whole debate? With some qualifications, I think the latter is true, and in this paper I shall try to show that the notion of rights, and indeed of human rights, is indispensable in any adequate discussion of policy which vitally affects human interests (and I suppose *foreign* policy necessarily falls under that description). Nevertheless, it is of course true that a great deal of talk about rights, and especially *human* rights, is both confused and confusing, these defects having no adverse effect, however, on the power of these concepts to warm the heart. It is desirable, therefore, to get these notions as clear as we can so that we can see what role they can and do play in any responsible thinking on the issues which constitute the theme of this conference.

Because philosophers like to get things clear, it's often mistakenly supposed by those who are aware of this predilection that the way to do this is to begin with definitions. However, if a definition of the phrase "human rights" is appropriate at all, it should come at the end of the enquiry, not at the beginning. Definitions have a comparatively minor role to play in philosophical analysis, and are normally useful only when technical terms, or terms of art, are being introduced. Then indeed there is an obligation to define such terms so that it will be clear what meaning the introducer of those terms wishes us to attach to them. But our task is not arbitrarily to give a meaning to the phrase "human rights" but to discover, if we can, what meaning this expression has. For the term "right" at least is not a term of art but the name of an ordinary non-technical concept, whose meaning has no sharp boundaries, and is in fact somewhat vague, though not necessarily any the worse for being that. The vast majority of the concepts we use in everyday life are fuzzy at the edges, their usefulness and versatility being partly a function of their very vagueness. Admittedly the expression "*human* rights" is much nearer to being a technical term, but it's the second of these two words with which we must begin.

The term "right" (understood as the singular of "rights") gets its meaning by virtue of the complicated web of relationships it has with other ordinary concepts and social practices, mainly in the fields of law and social morality. What we are looking for are the dominant conventions which determine what these relations are, though we must expect a certain degree of flexibility. Our verbal conventions are not governed by any *strict* rules, yet the rules are not so loose or so indeterminate as to license 'humpty-dumptyism'.[1] To use words that are not terms of art to mean whatever you want them to mean is to ensure that the communication breakdown will be complete.

What then does it mean to say "A has a right to do x"? I suggest that in most contexts of central importance it means something like the following: that (i) A is not required to justify doing x, and (ii) that no one is justified in preventing, or trying to prevent A from doing x. Conversely, when we say "A has no right to do x" we mean that A's doing x is *not* justifiable, and that someone (though not necessarily *anyone*) would be justified in preventing, or trying to prevent, A from doing x.

Though I'm confident that this is indeed a central use of the word "right", it's easy of course to think of usages which depart more or less from this pattern. But if my brief account of the central usage is roughly correct, then it will be easily understood why philosophers have seen an intimate connection between 'rights', 'claims' and 'justifications', and also why philosophers like Hart have argued that human or natural rights essentially have to do with the conditions under which the freedom both of individuals and institutions like governments, may and may not be justifiably restricted.[2]

Now although it is true that *if* A has a right to do x then it follows that A is not required to justify doing x, nevertheless A's having a right to do x may very well require justification. Conversely, if A has no right to do x then though no justification is required to stop A from doing x, the judgement that A has no right to do x may indeed require justification. I would go further and say that it must always require justification if one adopts the very reasonable principle that persons should be free to do anything they want to do unless there is good reason why they should be prevented. This principle, which we might call the presumption of freedom, I take to be analogous to the principle that persons should be presumed innocent until proven guilty. Neither principle is of course universally accepted, but I would want to argue (though not in this paper) that the embodiment of both these principles into the institutional framework of government is one of the marks of a civilized society.

Supposing then it is accepted that part of what it *means* to say "A has a right to do x" is that no one is justified in obstructing A from doing x, how can it be shown that A *does* have the right to do x? Well, *one* way of doing this is by showing that A is legally entitled to do x, which might simply involve pointing out that there is no positive law forbidding A from doing x. This is just another way of saying that A's right to do x is a legal right, and whether one has a legal right to do something is to be settled by consulting the appropriate legal authorities. Some philosophers have gone as far as saying that legal rights are the only rights there are, and that all talk of 'natural' rights not recognised by positive law is so much declamatory nonsense.

Against this I would argue that talk of 'natural' rights *may* sometimes be declamatory but it certainly need not be nonsense. The recognition that there are basic human rights, which are not necessarily endorsed by positive law, is perhaps one further mark of a civilized outlook. It is precisely because the most serious infringements of basic human rights have almost invariably been perfectly lawful that the failure to distinguish *legal* rights from what might be broadly classified as *moral* rights is worse than a mere philosophical confusion, for it has pernicious consequences.

We only need to be reminded that the trials of war criminals at Nuremburg would have been virtually unintelligible without the assumption that it is sometimes not enough to plead that one's actions were both permitted and even commanded by duly constituted lawful authority. Whatever the weaknesses and confusions there have been in some of the traditional theories of natural law, they have had at least this considerable merit, which they share with some of the traditional notions of natural rights, viz. that the laws of any nation without exception are a proper subject for moral scrutiny and moral criticism. We forget this at our peril.

But this is to anticipate a little, for the distinction between legal and moral rights is not identical with that between legal and 'human' or 'natural' rights. (Incidentally, I know of no useful distinction to be drawn between human and natural rights, so I'll use these terms indifferently.) In order therefore to help illuminate the notion of human rights we need to contrast them with what I shall describe as context-dependent rights. These latter may be either legal or moral (or both), and as the term suggests they owe their existence to some features of a more or less specific social context which, in part at least, creates them. In many instances, that is, if A has a right to do x it will be because of some conditions that apply to A's circumstances – for example, some agreement into which A has entered, a role that A occupies in the social structure, an office that A holds, a relation in which A stands, a task which A has accomplished, and so on. To establish therefore that A has a context-dependent right, reference must be made to the relevant positive laws, customs, institutionalised rules, social conventions and the like. Rights such as a chairman's right to exercise a casting vote, or a footballer's right to a place in the team, or the right of promisees to that which they were promised, or the right of a sailor to his tot of rum – these are all context-dependent rights which could be legal, moral, or perhaps neither (as in the case of the last-mentioned example).

I hope it is now clear then that if there are any human (or natural) rights then they are rights which simply lack this context-dependent feature. They are called 'human' not for the trivial reason that they are attributed only to humans, but because they are thought to belong to *all* humans at all times and in all places, beings that possess them simply by virtue of being members of the human race. Because such rights were never bestowed by particular circumstances, so, it is thought, particular circumstances can never take them away. Hence, they are frequently described as 'inalienable', 'imprescriptible', 'absolute' and 'self-evident'.

It is hardly surprising that passionate declarations on suitable public occasions that there are such human rights has been met by profound scepticism, if not derision, by many who have taken the trouble to reflect upon the subject in a cool hour. Bentham's famous remark that 'natural rights' is simple nonsense, and 'natural and imprescriptible rights' nonsense upon stilts,[3] has not been an isolated reaction, and until the last decade or so, modern philosophers don't appear to have taken the concept very seriously. However, I think it is now clear that the question "Are there any human rights?" deserves to be taken very seriously indeed. In trying to answer it, however, we don't have to confine ourselves to the acceptance or rejection of a package deal. For it's another question to ask whether human rights, if there are any, are in any sense inalienable, imprescriptible, absolute or self-evident.

Unfortunately, even when "human rights" is shorn of all its usual polysyllabic predicates, the question "Are there any?" to many people misleadingly suggests that to give a positive answer is to commit oneself to asserting the existence of mysterious metaphysical entities the proof of whose existence is likely to be difficult to produce. However, I suggested earlier in this paper that to say that A has a right to do x means, roughly speaking, that A is not required to justify doing x, and that no one is justified in preventing or trying to prevent A from doing x. If one says that there *are* human rights, therefore, one is simply endorsing the judgment that there are *some* things which *any* person should be free to do, and free to be, without any interference from anybody else, and without being liable to be called upon to give some kind of account. This way of putting it does I think make it clear that to declare a belief in the existence of human rights is to make a moral judgment, admittedly of a highly general sort, but nevertheless one which has a content of no small significance. For even a readiness to endorse this highly general moral judgment reveals a certain belief in the worth and dignity of human nature, as becomes clear as soon as one reflects on what it would mean to deny it. I suggest that to deny the existence of human rights is, in effect, to declare that persons ought to have only those freedoms which either they have managed to acquire through exploiting whatever opportunities they may have had to gain power or privilege, or else those which they possess by the gracious favour of others who happen to be in a position to bestow them, a favour which at any time may be withdrawn should these benefactors think it desirable. To believe that there *are* human rights, on the other hand, is to believe that there is, as it were, a buffer zone of freedom surrounding every human being which ought never to be encroached upon without proper justification. As Feinberg has put it,

> To think of oneself as the holder of rights is not to be unduly, but properly proud, to have that minimal self respect that is necessary to be worthy of the love and esteem of others.[4]

Another writer, Gregory Vlastos, makes a similar point when he stresses the close connection between the notions of human rights and human worth. The human worth of persons is, on this view, not a function of any special merits that they may happen to possess, but something which they have simply by virtue of being human individuals. To acknowledge the existence of human rights then is to have this concept of individual worth. It is to have a respect for persons as such.[5]

At this point, two questions arise, both of fundamental importance. First, is there any way of *showing* that those who deny the existence of human rights are mistaken? Second, even if the existence of human rights is granted, unless they are thought to be in some strong sense 'inalienable' or 'absolute' (surely a difficult position to defend), they will be regarded as being justifiably overriden in certain particular circumstances, and as everyone will have their own view as to what such circumstances are, won't this mean that assent to the existence of human rights will amount to little more than a pious verbal genuflexion in the direction of the United Nations Charter?

To the first of these questions I shall offer only the briefest of answers, for a proper answer to it would require a paper in itself. Once it is recognised that to assent to the existence of human rights is to make a moral judgment, then the question whether anyone who denies the existence of human rights can be shown to be mistaken becomes part of the more general question whether *any* moral judgment can be shown to be mistaken. This basic question concerning the place of reason and rational demonstration in ethics is much too complicated to discuss here. Let me simply register my protest at the widespread assumption, commonly thought to be self-evident, that once a dispute has been isolated as a moral or ethical dispute, there is no way in which that dispute can be resolved by rational argument. This is an uncritical dogma that deserves to be exposed as such, but I pass to the second question because, though it is less fundamental than the first, I suspect it is of more direct relevance to the theme of this seminar. For the pressing issue is not so much "How can we show that there are human rights to those who deny their existence?" but rather "To what does a belief in human rights commit us?". For it's relatively easy, especially at the official level, to get governments, politicians, organisers of protest movements, and the like, all to affirm their belief in fundamental human rights. What is difficult is to get clear what it would mean to take such a belief seriously.[6]

For example, can we speak of human rights as being 'inalienable' or 'imprescriptible'? Curiously enough, some of these who have wanted to apply these descriptions to rights have not wanted to deny that there are circumstances in which human rights can be justifiably overridden. They were ready to concede that there are imaginable circumstances in which justice would demand that a person's right to freedom of speech or even right to life must give way in the face of other moral considerations which are overriding.[7] Vlastos has remarked that in legal or quasi-legal contexts to speak of rights being 'inalienable' and 'imprescriptible' simply means that technically they cannot be signed away, or transferred by contract, and nor can they be lost by prescription, i.e. "in virtue of the time-hallowed possession of despotic power over them by a royal dynasty".[8] Nevertheless, because in certain circumstances the demands of justice may *require* that an individual's human rights be overridden, Vlastos prefers to speak of human rights being prima facie, by which he means not that human rights are apparent rather than real, but that circumstances may show that a particular individual's human rights on a particular occasion are prima facie only.[9] For perhaps they have committed a crime and therefore, at least temporarily, lost their right to freedom of movement; or perhaps they are in a crowded theatre and to exercise their freedom of speech by shouting "fire!" would cause a public disaster; or perhaps it's a national emergency and the exercising of any of their human rights would be likely to bring about a major catastrophe.

Few people who want to insist on the importance of human rights would deny that there *are* circumstances in which justice requires that those rights should be overridden. The point is, however, that if and when a right *is* overridden this has to be *justified*, and the grounds of the justification will have to relate to the *same* grounds which justify thc right, i.e. those considerations of human worth and respect for persons which we mentioned earlier. In other words, the *only* justification for overriding the human rights of individual persons is that allowing them to exercise those rights would be likely to jeopardise the human rights of others. It is worth emphasising that the grounds of such justification could *never* lie in the arbitrary power of some authority, legal or otherwise, for no authority created those rights in the first place. *This* is the point of describing them as 'inalienable' and 'imprescriptible'.[10] But these terms are misleading in so far as they suggest that even when individuals' human rights are justifiably overridden, nevertheless in *some* sense they *still* have those rights. It is surely an intolerable paradox to say that when criminals are justifiably imprisoned they still have the basic human right of freedom of movement, for if they *are* justifiably imprisoned, then it *follows* that freedom of movement is *not* one of their rights, human or otherwise.

This paradox is made more acceptable, if not removed entirely, by making use of Feinberg's distinction between a right and a claim.[11] To have a right is necessarily to have a claim and in the absence of counter-arguments to have a valid claim. No circumstances can make it false that the individual has a claim to (say) freedom of movement, but they may make it false that he has a valid claim, i.e. false that he has a right to freedom of movement in those circumstances. If I am justifiably imprisoned for some crime then at least for a period I do *not* have the right to be free. My right has been (temporarily) forfeited, but only because my claim to be free was successfully defeated.

In short then, declamatory talk about the inalienability and imprescriptibility of human rights does at least make the point that no government, no authority either human or divine, can take away human rights (though of course authorities can remove *legal* rights). Confusion is apt to arise at this point if we fail to keep clear the distinction between moral and legal rights. Human rights are a species of moral rights, and moral rights can be neither created nor destroyed by government action. If we speak then of a *government* overriding the human rights of individuals, this can only mean that the government in question is, either legally or illegally, making it impossible for those human rights to be recognised or exercised. It is just because it is not even logically possible for government action to 'take away' human rights that it makes sense to criticise a lawful government for failing to recognise and uphold human rights. The only way in which the overriding of a human right literally removes that right is when overriding it is *justified*, and the only justification for overriding the human rights of any person is that such action is morally demanded by the human rights of others.

Once this principle is clearly understood it will be seen that political leaders, nations and governments which on state occasions make a great show of upholding human rights ought to be aware that there is a price to pay. For example, it is not justifiable to deny persons the human right of freedom of speech on the grounds that allowing them to speak will do more harm than good. Considerations of what is in the general interest are not sufficient to override human rights. Upholding human rights may sometimes involve the slowing up of social progress, the lowering of the general standard of living, perhaps even an increase in the crime rate, for none of these things *necessarily* involves the violation of the human rights of others. If then it's our practice to appeal to the notion of human rights, we need to be aware of what is involved in taking rights seriously. This point is driven home with great effectiveness in an article of that title – 'Taking rights seriously' – by Ronald Dworkin, from whom I have learned much concerning the importance of human rights, and in particular the wider ramifications of recognising that only the competing human rights of individuals are sufficient to justify overriding the human rights of another individual.[12]

In this paper I have, I'm afraid, made little direct reference to the particular issues which constitute the theme of this conference. My aim has been to bring out some of the logical features of the concept of human rights in the hope that the better we understand the concept, the more responsible will be whatever use we wish to make of it. But I want to stress, what is no doubt obvious anyway, that I have done no more than offer a preliminary, tentative sketch. The subject, I'm afraid, is even more complicated than my treatment of it might have suggested. Furthermore I have deliberately avoided any attempt at making a *list* of human rights even though I hope I have left it in no doubt that I regard their recognition as of the first importance. Though this sounds paradoxical, even perhaps irresponsible, at this point I confess I don't know how to remedy the situation, for I would be far from confident just what should be included in the list. If pressed I would be inclined to follow Hart's suggestion that human rights have essentially got something to do with freedom, and that violations of human rights therefore always involve the violation of certain basic freedoms.[13] Earlier in this paper I drew attention to the close connection between human rights and the notions of individual worth, human dignity and respect for persons. Now if we reflect on what it means to be a person then, whatever else we may want to say, I think we *must* say that to be a person essentially involves having the capacity to perform intentional actions. Having the capacity to form intentions and purposes and to act upon them seems to be a sine qua non of being a fully human person. If this is so, it is hardly surprising that a denial of human rights is fundamentally the restriction and impairment of that very capacity which perhaps more than anything else constitutes our humanity.

Notes

1. "'When I use a word,' Humpty Dumpty said in rather a scornful tone, 'it means just what I choose it to mean – neither more nor less.'" Lewis Carroll, *Through the Looking Glass*.

2. E.g. Vlastos and Hart.
3. Bentham.
4. Feinberg, p. 464.
5. Vlastos, pp. 86ff.
6. For a particularly valuable discussion, see Dworkin.
7. This seems to be true of Locke, for example. See Vlastos, p. 81f.
8. Vlastos, p. 83.
9. Vlastos, p. 82.
10. The description of human rights as 'absolute' and 'self-evident' is, I think, less defensible.
11. Feinberg, pp. 461ff.
12. Dworkin.
13. Hart.

Bibliography

Bentham, Jeremy. *Anarchical Fallacies* (selections reprinted in Melden, to which page numbers refer).

Dworkin, R. 'Taking Rights Seriously' *New York Review of Books*, December, 1970.

Feinberg, Joel. 'The Nature and Value of Rights' in *Concepts in Social and Political Philosophy*, ed. Richard E. Flathman (Macmillan, N.Y., 1973).

Hart, H.L.A. 'Are there any Natural Rights?' *The Philosophical Review*, Vol. 64, 1955 (reprinted in Melden).

Melden, A.I. (ed.) *Human Rights* (Wadsworth, Belmont, Calif., 1970).

Vlastos, Gregory. 'Justice and Equality' in *Social Justice*, ed. R.B. Brandt (selections reprinted in Melden, to which page numbers refer).

Postscript

Michael Cullen, formerly Minister of Finance under the Labour government led by Helen Clark, was among those who attended this lecture. I don't recall whether he made any critical comments.

7
The Moral Responsibility of the Scientist

Some of the things I have to say in this paper will, I suspect, meet with a sceptical (if not a hostile) reaction, so I'm glad to begin with what is utterly non-controversial, perhaps even truistic. It is simply the platitudinous observation that Man, by developing a sophisticated technology made possible by the invention of scientific method, has acquired the capacity radically to change the world in which he lives. He has already changed it so profoundly that no one can know the full extent and significance of these changes. Moreover, particularly over the last two or three decades, the rate by which technological prowess has increased has been so rapid that even the best informed can only make wild guesses at what specifically Man might do, and has already done, both to himself and his environment. But in relatively general terms, we know that Man now can turn what we have learned to call the biosphere into a living hell, a process which some think we may have already irreversibly set in motion.

However, stated just like that these platitudes are dangerously misleading, for when we refer to 'Man' as a species and go on to talk about what he has done or is likely to do, we are apt to forget that Man as a species has not intentionally done anything. He hasn't intentionally developed a technology, intentionally polluted the environment, or overpopulated the world – nor of course has he done these things unintentionally. It makes no sense to blame Man for what he has done, nor would it make any better sense to excuse him for it, or to congratulate him. This is, of course, because Man as a species doesn't literally 'do' anything at all. Man is not even a corporate body in the sense in which a committee or a nation is a corporate body, for Man has no corporate will. A committee or a nation, if it has the appropriate institutional apparatus, can express something like a corporate will, and hence there's an important sense in which a committee or a nation can be held responsible (in the sense of being 'answerable') for its actions. It is nonsense to hold Man responsible (in this sense) for anything. Only individual men and women, or corporate social institutions made up of individual men and women, are literally responsible. But Man is not a corporate social institution.

So if we want to talk about 'Man's Responsibility for Nature' (to quote the title of a recent book) we need to remember that this can only be a figure of speech – an elliptical way of referring to the responsibility of individuals. Similarly, if we use the term 'scientist' to refer to a particular species of academic, then it's not literally true that 'the scientist' can be said to have a social responsibility. Only individual scientists can be held to have a social responsibility. Of course a particular scientific society or institution may properly be held to have a social responsibility if it has the appropriate institutional apparatus for expressing its corporate will. But the collection of all the individuals who belong to the species of academic known as scientists do not form a corporate social institution any more than do the sum total of all human beings.

The point of these preliminary remarks is that if we are going to raise questions about the social or moral responsibility of the scientist, we need to remember that such responsibility, if it can be ascribed at all, will have to be ascribed to individuals, or at least to corporate social institutions. Even when we hold a social institution responsible for its actions, we are ascribing responsibility to those individuals who execute its corporate will, as well as indirectly to those who have delegated their individual responsibility to their society's executive. Therefore, if we find it appropriate to talk about the social or moral responsibility of the scientist, it will only be because it is appropriate to hold particular individuals responsible for the actions which they perform in their capacity as scientists.

Though I shall argue that it is appropriate to regard individual scientists as having a moral responsibility for what they do as scientists, it's not obvious that they should be so regarded. For though the advance of science is certainly partly responsible for the technological revolution which among other things has resulted in massive pollution of our planet, it doesn't follow from this that some individual scientists, let alone any group of scientists collectively, are even partly morally responsible for that pollution; any more than it follows from the fact that the mosquito is partly responsible for the spread of malaria, that the mosquito is morally responsible for spreading that disease.

The point to note, of course, is that the word "responsible" is ambiguous. The statement "A is responsible for the event B" can mean simply that A is the cause of B, or it can mean that A is answerable for bringing B about. Essential to the latter concept of responsibility, but not the former, is the notion of intentional action having foreseen or foreseeable consequences, This explains how science can be responsible for pollution, in the sense of being an indirect cause of it, without it following from this that any individual scientist or group of scientists, or even all scientists collectively are even partly responsible (answerable) for this evil. Hence, whether and to what extent individual scientists, or scientific communities, can properly be held morally responsible for any of the benefits or evils of the technological revolution is an open question, and is not settled in advance by the platitudinous observation that science is in a large measure responsible for (i.e. the cause of) those benefits and evils.

How far then and in what sense is it appropriate to regard scientists as bearing a moral responsibility for the effects of science on society? In trying to answer this question I am going to assume that there are at least some human actions for which it is appropriate to hold individuals morally responsible. This of course is a controversial assumption, for some versions of determinism or mechanism entail that no one can ever appropriately be held morally responsible for his actions. If such theories are correct, then a fortiori no scientist bears any moral responsibility whatever. Though I think such theories are false, attempting to show that they are would belong to a different paper. I shall simply assume that it is possible that at least some scientists on at least some occasions bear a moral responsibility for their actions in their capacity as scientists. This might seem to be an excessively cautious claim, but I believe the caution is justified. This is because there is usually a considerable distance, as it were, between the pursuit of scientific knowledge and the application of such knowledge in the form of technology. Those who are more or less directly involved with deciding in what ways, and with what safeguards and controls, scientific technology should be implemented in society are often not themselves scientists, and even when they are their voice is often a small one and is not necessarily the determining factor in a political decision. Those who are actually engaged in scientific research, and who may be in a position to foresee, however dimly, that application of the results of their research may be potentially beneficial or harmful to society to a very considerable degree, are seldom in a position to have any direct say as to how (if at all) their discoveries should be put to practical use. Moreover, the very distance which separates their work from its practical application means that they are not always well placed to judge just what its beneficial or harmful effects are likely to be. A's research may be potentially harmful only when combined with B's research, yet neither A nor B may be aware of this at the time. Remote consequences of our actions are notoriously difficult to foresee, and normally it's not appropriate to hold anyone responsible for the consequences of their actions if they were neither foreseen nor foreseeable. It would be absurd to hold Rutherford morally responsible for Hiroshima. In general the more remote the consequences are from the action which produced them, the less appropriate it is to speak of them as being the consequences of that action, for that action will be but one of a myriad of contributing causal factors which go to make up the causal ancestry of these consequences. Mother Goose's rhyme about the battle that was lost "all for the want of a horse shoe nail" is a useful reminder that apparently trivial factors may sometimes play a decisive role in national events, but it would indeed be a naïve historian who would lay the moral responsibility for a nation's defeat on the shoulders of some unknown careless blacksmith.

Nevertheless, even when we allow full weight to all these cautionary qualifications, I believe there is no doubt that morally sensitive scientists are rightly aware that, by virtue of the kind of work in which they are professionally engaged, they bear a considerable load of moral responsibility. Granted, they may not often be in a position to foresee even in vague outline the social consequences which are likely to result from the practical application of the fruits of their work. But they know, on the best inductive grounds, that in the past some of the most innocent looking research has led to technological applications whose effects have turned out to be socially dangerous to a frightening degree. Let us also grant that there is a bright side to this picture as well as a gloomy side. Science can, and has, led to technological applications whose beneficial social consequences have been enormous. Indeed, in the 19th century, it was the benefits of science for mankind which, for many, dominated the picture, so that dedicated scientists were in the happy situation of having a double incentive. Not only did they have the intrinsic interest and fascination of scientific discovery for its own sake to motivate them, but also, should their zeal for work ever begin to flag, there was always the encouraging thought of those unknown benefits to mankind to which their discoveries might well lead. Even when I was an undergraduate (which is not all that long ago) when the evil purposes to which scientific technology can be put had been made appallingly apparent by the Second World War, I remember my psychology professor saying, somewhat smugly, that every scientific discovery is likely to have an equal potentiality for both good and evil, and that therefore it is the responsibility of others to decide what use should be made of scientific knowledge: it is the scientist's duty simply to produce it. Such a view nowadays is dangerously myopic and over-simplified. The potentiality of science for good and evil is asymmetrical, for without underrating in the least the benefits to mankind which science has made possible, the world is now so situated that, unlike the good effects, the harmful effects of technology tend to increase exponentially – which simply means that things can get very very bad, very very quickly. It is the extreme urgency of the social dangers arising from the misuse of science which, more than anything else, aggravates the burden of moral responsibility which scientists carry.

Awareness of the moral urgency of the situation has produced a dilemma for scientists which, historically speaking, is comparatively new. For now, much more than in the past, they are caught in a conflict of duties. On the one hand they have a professional duty as scientists and academics to follow the argument wherever it may lead and to make freely available to all the results of their research, and on the other hand they have a duty as human beings to respect life, and human life in particular. Just how serious this dilemma is will only be fully appreciated by those who are as sensitive to the importance of *both* these duties as they are to the fact of the accelerating rate at which they are becoming more and more incompatible. Any compromise with the first strikes at the very heart of science as an academic discipline, for that there should be no prohibited fields of enquiry, no concealing of the truth, is intrinsic to its very nature. Any compromise with the second duty, on the other hand, strikes at the very heart of human existence and can be ignored only at the cost of ignoring the truism that a scientist is a human being.

Though, for historical reasons, this moral dilemma which I've been describing, is comparatively speaking a new one, what is not new of course is that human beings are faced with a moral dilemma. In the remainder of this paper, therefore, I propose to make some remarks about what it is to be faced with a moral dilemma and I shall try to dispose of some fundamental confusions concerning the nature of morality which are apt to get in the way of our arriving at responsible conclusions on moral issues.

Postscript

This is part one of a contribution I made in 1982 to a symposium sponsored by the Centre for Continuing Education at Victoria University, Wellington on the subject of 'Moral Decision-making in Public Affairs.' The text or notes for part two, on the nature of moral dilemmas, are missing but what I wrote in part one still seems worth preserving. (Of course I would now much prefer the expression "Humankind" in place of "Man".)

8

Miracles and God's Existence

I

Suppose I have a friend (whose good sense on most matters I respect), who takes seriously the possibility that some at least of the miracle stories associated with the origin of the Christian religion are substantially true. He does not say that he knows them to be true, but given his belief in the existence of an almighty, all loving creator-god, he sees no reason to think it impossible that they are, and considerable reason for thinking one or two of them highly probable. He regards those who claim that (say) the resurrection of Jesus could not have happened as being unreasonably dogmatic, and as displaying an attitude of mind more appropriate to the eighteenth and nineteenth centuries than the latter half of the twentieth century. To rule out the very possibility of the truth of such stories on a priori grounds seems to him to manifest a simplistic philosophical faith which is at least as naïve and arbitrary, and perhaps considerably more arrogant, than his own religious faith. Could he be right?

I think it has to be admitted that a priori arguments against miracles often do have a certain air of simplistic absurdity about them, and yet, arguably, they are the only arguments against miracles which could be of any philosophical interest. Moreover, it is not clear that they are necessarily either simplistic or absurd, as Hume's essay 'Of Miracles' abundantly testifies.[1] The first part of this paper is another attempt to set out such an argument, whose affinities with the Humean argument will be obvious, but which is expressed in a form less vulnerable to the standard objections which have been made against Hume.

Suppose I am sceptical about miracles. My scepticism can manifest itself in either of two ways. On the one hand, I may be in no doubt that if an event identified under a certain description were to take place it would certainly be a miracle, and yet be extremely sceptical whether any event of that kind has ever actually occurred. On the other hand, I may have little or no doubt that an extremely unusual and remarkable event, identified under a certain description, actually did take place, and yet be extremely sceptical whether that event should be correctly described as 'a miracle'. That is, my scepticism can be directed either at the historical question or at the conceptual question. The essential thrust of the Humean a priori argument against miracles is this: with respect to any alleged miracle, the extent to which evidence can show that scepticism relating to the historical question is unjustified will necessarily constitute the very same evidence for showing that scepticism relating to the conceptual question is justified. Conversely, any evidence which showed that it would be unreasonable to be sceptical concerning the conceptual question would constitute the very same evidence for justifying scepticism concerning the historicity of the alleged event.

One obvious way to refute the Humean dilemma is to provide at least one counter-example in the form of a description of some logically possible event, set in logically possible circumstances of a particular kind, such that if an event answering to this description were to occur in such circumstances, it would be unreasonable for anyone to deny that a miracle had actually taken place. Whether there has in fact been an event and set of circumstances satisfying those conditions would of course be a separate question, but all we need in order to destroy the a priori argument is just one logically possible, hypothetical, counter-example. Then the question whether any miracles have in fact occurred, or might occur in the future, would at least be an open one, and (at least in principle) an answerable one.

In order to refute Hume, it is not sufficient simply to point out that it is surely logically possible that water should turn into wine, or a rod turn into a serpent, or a dead man rise from the dead. Incredibly, some have taken Hume to be denying this, and have taken him to task for so conveniently forgetting his own philosophical principles. After all it was Hume himself who insisted that

> the mind can always conceive . . . any event to follow upon another; whatever we conceive is possible, at least in a metaphysical sense.[2]

Hume would certainly not deny that it is logically possible for a dead man to rise from the dead. Nor would he deny that, when expressed in general terms, the notion of a dead man rising from the dead is a notion of a truly miraculous event. What he would deny is that it is logically possible for anyone to have good reason simultaneously to believe both that such an event had in fact taken place, and that that particular event was indeed a miracle. Exactly why he would deny this is not all that obvious. Still less obvious is whether he is justified in denying it. But that he does deny it, and that the basis of his denial is what he takes to be the particular logical relations which hold between the concepts of miracle and evidence (or good reason) I propose to assume without argument. My main concern is to see whether the denial can be justified.

Is the concept of miracle such as to exclude the possibility that anything could count as evidence that a miracle had occurred? Is it self-contradictory to speak of a well-attested miraculous event? This will in part depend on what we understand by the term 'miracle' and, in particular, whether we regard miracles as being events which are necessarily inexplicable in naturalistic terms. Hume had no doubts on this point. He made it clear that in his view no event, no matter how remarkable or unusual, should properly be termed a miracle if we could explain its occurrence, either now or in the future, in terms of the natural world. This is because if the occurrence of such an event is just what an adequate knowledge of nature would have led one to expect, then there would be no reason to regard it as specially revelatory of some divine power. On the other hand, an event normally regarded as a purely natural event (such as a shower of rain) would nevertheless truly be a miracle if its timing was such that it occurred in answer to some human need or command, provided of course that there was no suspicion that such timing was purely accidental. In all this I think that Hume was correct and I shall express the point by making it a defining characteristic of miracles that they be a species of anomalous events. By 'anomalous event' I shall mean an event which is incompatible with, and permanently inexplicable in terms of, scientific theory (and hence a 'violation' of the laws of nature).

How, if at all, could we ever be justified in regarding an event as 'anomalous' in the defined sense? For although it is easy to think of logically possible events which, if they were to occur, would certainly be inexplicable in terms of current scientific theory, it is less obvious that there could be any particular event, no matter how unusual or bizarre, which we would be justified in regarding as being permanently inexplicable in scientific or naturalistic terms. Even if some actual events will in fact permanently remain inexplicable in naturalistic terms (as seems quite probable), on the face of it this would be no more than a purely contingent fact. How could we have any reason to say of any particular event that it will never be explained naturalistically? In other words, according to this line of reasoning, no matter what extraordinary events were to take place, it would never be reasonable to believe that any laws of nature had been violated, and hence it would never be reasonable to believe that a miracle had occurred. Apparently anomalous events can never imply any more than that some of the laws of nature were not what we took them to be.

It has sometimes been suggested that the simple and adequate reply to this line of reasoning is that it takes more than a single, non-repeated counterexample to destroy a scientific law, or even to warrant some modification to be made to a law.[3] Unless an obvious exception to a law (or what is taken to be one) is experimentally repeatable, the scientific and explanatory status of that law is not impugned. It is not self-contradictory to speak of a truly anomalous event.

While this reply is adequate as far as it goes, it leaves untouched the much more formidable problem of whether we could ever have reason to believe that a truly anomalous event had occurred, even if it is granted that such events are logically possible. For it would seem that there is no way that we can have reason to believe that some particular event has taken place except by making use of inductive evidence. That is to say, any claim that we have evidence that an anomalous event has occurred, would itself necessarily depend on the tacit assumption that events in the natural world in some sense constitute a vast network of exceptionless regularities. Therefore, because nothing could count as evidence for an event's occurrence without our making assumptions not only concerning what has happened in the past but also about what must happen, as well as what cannot possibly happen, it would seem that to claim that we have evidence that what cannot possibly happen nevertheless has happened would involve us in a manifest contradiction.

It is this argument which constitutes the essence of the Humean argument against miracles and the first to see this clearly was Antony Flew.[4] The latest follower of this line of interpretation is P. S. Wadia who puts the point in this way:

> No one can be justified in both thinking that it is reasonable to accept beliefs arrived at inductively and thinking, at the same time, that it may sometimes be reasonable to believe in the occurrence of a miracle.

He argues that those who claim that

> it is not unreasonable to believe that 'on occasion the physically impossible occurs' cannot do so without at some point in their argument being forced to appeal to the very conception of rationality that they must begin by rejecting.[5]

Unfortunately, Wadia himself confuses the issue when at another point he insists that "it is certainly logically possible for someone to be in a position reasonably to conclude that the balance of evidence proves that a law of nature has been violated. But it is simply irrational to believe that anyone in fact ever was, or ever will be, in such a position."[6] It is irrational, he thinks, in the same sense as it would be irrational for someone to believe that something was physically possible merely because it happened to be logically possible.

But this is to miss the essentially a priori nature of the Humean argument. For although it is not logically impossible that a violation of a law of nature should occur, what is logically impossible (according to the Humean argument) is that we could have evidence sufficient to make it reasonable to believe that such a thing had happened. For if the only way in which we can have evidence that a violation of the laws of nature has occurred is by assuming that the laws of nature are never violated, then clearly it is logically impossible for us to have any such evidence.[7]

The force of this argument becomes clearer once we realize that it is impossible for anyone even to appear to have any reason to accept a miracle-story unless they share the common presupposition that Nature behaves in a law-like manner. For example, certain well-known New Testament miracle stories would not have been believed by anyone who did not also believe the following: that no man could have endured the events which Jesus endured on Good Friday without really dying; that it is not possible for everyone at a wedding feast to be unable to taste the difference between wine and water; that 5,000 people could not all be mistaken in thinking that they had had a good lunch, if each had had no more than 1/1000 part of a loaf plus 1/2500 part of a small fish. And so on. Without these inductively based assumptions concerning what is strictly impossible there would be no reason to think that any laws of nature had been broken at all. But oddly enough these assumptions are themselves valid only if it is true that the laws of nature cannot be broken. Or so it would seem.

This argument holds not merely against any alleged evidence for miracles which depends on the testimony of witnesses. It has often been suggested that because Hume confines himself to discussing the value of evidence supplied by the testimony of witnesses, he would find it very embarrassing if he were actually to see a miracle performed before his very eyes. However, in so far as even the direct observation of events constitutes evidence for their occurrence only on the condition that we invoke certain inductively based assumptions connected with perception, it would make no difference to the Humean argument to imagine that we were actually eye-witnesses to an alleged miracle. Even if we were eye witnesses (Hume might have argued), to avoid an inconsistent employment of the concept of evidence we would have to conclude either that the turning of water into wine (for example) did not really constitute an anomalous event (and hence was only apparently a miracle), or else the turning of water into wine was not what we had observed after all but some other event which we mistakenly thought was an instance of water turning into wine. That is, at least for 'the wise and learned', it would be reasonable to be sceptical either about the conceptual question (was it really a miracle?) or about the historical question (was it really a case of water turning into wine?).

II

I now want to argue that, Hume's argument to the contrary notwithstanding, not only does it make sense to suppose that we could have grounds for thinking that a physically impossible event has occurred but that we could even have grounds for thinking that an anomalous event has occurred, i.e. an event which would remain permanently inexplicable in naturalistic or scientific terms.[8] In order to show this, let us imagine that you, the reader, along with a handful of other witnesses, are present in my study as I write this paper. You know that, in the course of writing it, the pencil I am using will not turn into a lizard, since such an event is physically impossible. But suppose two minutes from now it nevertheless happened. Of course, even if you think you saw it happen you would be right (i.e. justified) not to believe it, for after all, we have all seen rabbits being pulled out of empty hats. Nevertheless, we can easily imagine that we could satisfy ourselves that it was not an illusion or a clever conjuring trick provided we had full opportunity beforehand to check out the pencil as well as the room, the condition of the observers, etc., and (after the event) the lizard. Though such checks might need to be very elaborate, it seems hard to maintain that no matter how thorough and meticulous they were it would always be more reasonable to conclude that the pencil had not turned into a lizard after all. Admittedly, we might be in some legitimate doubt as to whether that was the correct way of describing the event. But even if we preferred to say that at a particular moment the pencil ceased to exist and at precisely that same moment a lizard came into existence in its place, we would still be faced with a physically impossible event having happened. And this would mean that we were wrong in predicting that it would not happen. Furthermore, though we claimed we knew it would not happen, if it did then obviously we could not have known that it would not. But this does not mean that we were not justified in claiming that we knew that it would not, for the simple reason that this knowledge-claim is about as well-grounded as any empirical knowledge-claim can possibly be. If we are not justified in claiming to know that pencils cannot turn into lizards then we are not justified in claiming to know anything. I think we can go further and say that if such an event were to happen, then not only would this not impugn our justification for claiming to know that it would not: it might not even impugn our justification for regarding such an event as anomalous. I grant that it is not so easy to see how we could be justified in regarding an event as being permanently inexplicable in naturalistic or scientific terms. For on the face of it, if an event has actually occurred, and we know that it has, then we would expect some sort of explanation as to why it had occurred to be in the offing. But could we have grounds for concluding that no matter how much evidence we were to gather, and no matter what should turn out to be the future evolution of science, a scientific explanation would never be forthcoming? Perhaps not, if this pencil turned into a lizard simply in the course of my writing this paper. But I think we can conceive of circumstances such that we would be justified not only in concluding that a physically impossible event had indeed taken place, but also that that event was rightly to be regarded as anomalous in the defined sense. For let us now suppose that the turning of the pencil into a lizard occurred in a context more recognizably religious than the present context. Let us suppose that some popularly acclaimed holy man or prophet declared that he was a chosen prophet of Mazda the god of light, and that he would call upon his god to show his power by turning a pencil into a lizard. We would again need to check with meticulous thoroughness that all possibility of fraud and trickery was ruled out, but provided that there were no limitations at all placed on our checking investigations, both before and after the event, there seems no reason to suppose that we could not be rationally satisfied on that point. Let us further suppose that not only did our holy man succeed in bringing it about that a pencil turned into a lizard, but also that he performed a dozen or so other feats of an equally bizarre and 'impossible' nature, in each case the event occurring only after he had called upon his god Mazda to show his power. Finally, lest there still remain any stiff -necked sceptics in his audience, our prophet invites members of the crowd of witnesses to name a half-dozen or more equally impossible events which he will ask Mazda to cause to come to pass at various specified intervals after the prophet's own death, and behold these events all do subsequently happen, and at precisely the times predicted.[9] What I am suggesting is that if a series of events each as bizarre as a pencil turning into a lizard were to take place in this sort of context and under these circumstances, then the rational conclusion to draw would be that they had been caused to come about by the power of some invisible agent who had the capacity to understand verbally expressed requests as well as the capacity to perform intentional actions. Moreover, if events of this sort were never known to occur except in response to requests to Mazda, and then only by a few people conspicuous for their piety and sincerity and their devotion to Mazda, I suggest it would be unreasonable to look for some ways of modifying scientific theory to accommodate and 'explain' such events. It might just be conceivable that if my pencil just happened to turn into a lizard in the course of the writing of this paper, science might one day explain it in terms of the effect of some sort of freak radiation phenomenon or the like that occurs maybe once every billion years or so.

But even to begin to explain scientifically a whole series of equally 'impossible' events, occurring in the quasi-religious circumstances I have described, would not merely require a modification of some branches of scientific theory. It would demand something like the dismantling of the whole scientific edifice altogether. By far the simpler and more rational thing to do would be not to seek to make any adjustments at all to scientific theory but to posit the existence of some personal or quasi-personal being who had the capacity to understand certain human requests and the power to bring about the occurrence of certain events (normally regarded as physically impossible) in response to those requests. In short, were such events to take place in the manner and circumstances I have described, then though we would turn out to be wrong in thinking that they would not happen, we would not turn out to be unjustified both in claiming them to be physically impossible and in describing them as anomalous. In particular, our grounds for regarding them as anomalous (in the defined sense) would be as firm as any other empirical claim whatever. Of course it would still be logically possible that we should be mistaken in so describing them, but this would no more show that we are not justified in regarding a pencil turning into a lizard as impossible and anomalous than the mere logical possibility of its occurring would show that we are not justified in claiming that we know that it will not.

There is an obvious objection to this line of argument, arising from considerations mentioned earlier. The a priori argument which I outlined in Part I implied (among other things) that it is not legitimate to consider what we should conclude if a physically impossible event were to occur, since nothing will count as inductive evidence for the occurrence of an event unless we presuppose that true laws of nature cannot be broken, or, in other words, that the physically impossible cannot occur. Once we allow that an event's being physically impossible is not sufficient to rule out all possibility (save the logical possibility) of its occurring, then the concept of evidence has become detached from its proper conceptual framework and only nonsense can result.

I believe that our elaborate counterexample has shown up the essential weakness of this objection. Essentially, the a priori argument depends for its plausibility on an oversimplified account of what constitutes the nature of evidence. For although it is certainly true that in our imagined counterexample the whole paraphernalia involved in checking for deception and illusion presupposes that the relevant laws associated with those checking procedures remain intact, it does not presuppose that all the laws of nature should remain inviolable. Of course, abstracted from a particular context, it would be arbitrarily inconsistent to invoke the inviolability of one law of nature as grounds for declaring another to have been violated. But the particular context which we described made it clear that the simplest, most economical, most reasonable explanation available to us was essentially a teleological explanation, made possible by positing the existence of some kind of quasi-personal invisible agent as being the cause of that particular pattern of extraordinary events. Just positing the existence of an invisible intentional agent would of course make no sense unless we presupposed that most of the laws of nature had not been violated, but on that assumption it is possible to explain the violation of some laws of nature (in this case relating to physics and biology) by positing the existence of an intentional agent whose actions unify the observed series of anomalous events. Moreover, there is nothing irrational about a teleological explanation as such, given that almost all ordinary explanations of human behaviour are of this sort. The point is that just which laws of nature we regard as having been violated and which we assume have remained intact, as well as the inference we draw concerning the nature of the intentional agent whose existence is posited, are all judgments controlled by the principles of economy and simplicity. The number of laws of nature assumed to have been violated, as well as the extent to which we enrich our ontology, would need to be no more than is minimally required to explain our observational experiences.

In brief then, I have argued that the a priori argument which I have attributed to Hume fails. Suitably described counterexamples show that we could find ourselves in circumstances in which it would be reasonable to conclude not only that a series of anomalous events had occurred, but also that these were brought about by some invisible or rather physically undetectable agent whose intentional actions were a necessary condition for their having taken place. In such circumstances, not only would a wise and learned man be justified in concluding that a series of miracles had occurred, but also a man would hardly deserve to be called wise and learned unless he drew this conclusion.

I hardly need add that whether in fact anyone has ever been in circumstances that would justify this inference is a very different question which I do not propose to pursue in this paper. Suffice it to say that if Hume's argument is interpreted not as an a priori argument to show that it is impossible to have grounds for believing a miracle to have occurred, but as an a posteriori argument to show the extreme improbability of our ever having such grounds, I think his argument inescapable. The elaborate stage-setting for the series of events which constituted our counterexample to the Humean a priori argument is an essential part of the refutation of that argument. We are totally mistaken if we regard it as heavy artillery which may be necessary as a weapon against the hardened sceptic, but which results in overkill when directed against the doubts of the ordinary reasonable man of faith. When any miracle story is presented to us, if we are reasonable we surely must, as Hume insists, consider whether it is more probable that the report of the event is due to human error, self-deception, fraud and the like than due to the event's actually having happened. Or again, whether it is more probable that the anomalous character of the event implied in its description is due to human ignorance of nature's ways than that something has occurred which really will remain permanently inexplicable in naturalistic terms. Which of each pair of these alternatives is the more probable with regard to the miracle stories contained in the extant literature of the great world religions seems to me to be beyond reasonable doubt.

At this point it is relevant to return to the remarks I attributed to my Christian friend at the beginning of this paper. For it will no doubt be objected that what is considered probable with regard to miracles will very much depend on whether one already has a belief in an almighty personal god. Given such a belief, the probability of any miracle story's being true will depend not merely on the amount and quality of the relevant evidence, but also (and just as importantly) on whether the alleged miracle was of such a nature as could be fittingly attributed to the kind of god believed in. The probability of any particular miracle story (it will be said) is bound to be assessed very differently by one who already believes in an almighty, personal god than by someone who rejects such a belief. And such a discrepancy between the assessment of probabilities would seem only reasonable.

Except for one difficulty. How we could have any grounds at all for this prior belief in a personal god apart from evidence provided by a series of miracles is not easy to see. For it is surely part of the very concept of a personal being that such a being perform actions, at least from time to time. There could be no reason for attributing personal qualities to a being who literally never does anything, and never has done anything at all. It might be claimed that the very existence of an ordered universe is evidence for the existence of a supremely intelligent, personal being who designed it. Certainly if some version of the design argument could be shown to be sound, then conceivably this might provide us with some sort of foundational belief in a personal god which would make the occurrence of miracles initially more probable. Unfortunately the design argument is pretty widely agreed to be fallacious, justifiably in my view. In particular, those who appeal to a religious revelation are usually as convinced as anyone that neither the design argument nor any other traditional buttress of a natural theology can provide us with grounds for a belief in a personal god. What is less often appreciated is that this leaves miracles, and miracles alone, as the only possible foundation for a belief in a personal god. For if there can be no reason to believe in a personal god unless we have reason to think such a god has acted, then the only evidence for his (or her) actions that we could have would be through our experiencing the occurrence of events which we had reason to believe were anomalous. This is because unless events are seen to be truly anomalous it would be totally unreasonable to posit the existence of an invisible personal being to explain them. And this point would apply not merely to alleged events which are in principle publicly observable (like water turning into wine, or rods turning into serpents), but also and more significantly to all privately experienced events associated with personal religious experiences. For unless we have grounds for regarding these events as miraculous, there would be no reason to suppose that their explanation could not in principle, and therefore perhaps eventually in fact, be provided in purely naturalistic terms, thereby rendering otiose any reference to the existence of a personal god.

My conclusion is that we do not know a priori that no miracles have occurred, for we can specify in broad outline what sort of occurrences in what sort of circumstances would make it reasonable to conclude that a miracle had indeed happened. Nevertheless, the kinds of circumstances that would justify this are themselves so fantastic that the likelihood of their ever obtaining is itself something we know, on inductive grounds, to be extremely remote. And yet, assuming all versions of the design argument to be unsound, the only grounds we could have for belief in the existence of a personal god would be the occurrence of a fair number of well-attested miracles.

My Christian friend, therefore, was right to take the question of miracles seriously. Perhaps his mistake was in not taking it seriously enough.

Notes

1. David Hume, 'Of Miracles'. *Enquiry Concerning the Human Understanding*, ed. L.A. Selby-Bigge.
2. David Hume, *An Abstract of a Treatise of Human Nature*, ed. J. M. Keynes and P. Straffa (Cambridge University Press, 1938), pp. 13–14 (italics in original).
3. See, for example, Ninian Smart, *Philosophers and Religious Truth* (London: SCM Press, 1964), pp. 54f.
4. See his classic discussion of Hume's essay in Antony Flew, *Hume's Philosophy of Belief* (London: Routledge and Kegan Paul, 1961), ch. 8.
5. P. S. Wadia, 'Miracles and Common Understanding', *Philosophical Quarterly* 26, No. 102 (January 1976), p. 76.
6. P. S. Wadia, op. cit., p. 74.
7. Though at this point he falters, I regard Wadia's discussion as a whole as the most illuminating interpretation of what Hume was on about since the publication of Flew's book referred to in note 4.
8. In this section I owe a great debt to P. Diehtl, 'On Miracles', *Philosophical Quarterly* 51 No. 2 (April 1968), pp. 130–134.

9. More elaborate safeguards against the possible future discovery of covering-law explanations of such events are suggested by Diehtl, op. cit., pp. 131–132.

Postscript

I continue to be amazed that Hume's devastating critique of the concept of miracle in the context of religious belief is virtually ignored by religious believers. However, his essay has also important implications for the philosophy of history, and in particular what constitutes the notion of historical evidence. It is no accident that Hume was, in his day, perhaps more famous as a historian than as a philosopher.

I regard Flew's elucidation of the force of Hume's argument as especially valuable. I once met Flew at a philosophy conference and took the opportunity to ask him if he would like to read my essay, which he did. He agreed with the drift of my argument and commented that my reference to the limitations of Hume's critique had not before occurred to him.

I regard my concluding paragraphs as constituting a particular difficulty for those who want to retain a belief in a personal creator-God, but who ignore the fact that if the only evidence we have concerning God's attributes is God's creation, then the mechanism of evolution by natural selection portrays a God who is utterly indifferent to animal and human suffering.

9
The Morality of Nuclear Deterrence

Central to the policy of nuclear deterrence (ND) is the threat to respond to nuclear attack with nuclear retaliation. The fundamental moral question concerning the ND policy is whether this threat is morally justifiable. That is the question I want to discuss.

An adequate account of the ND policy would of course be complex and lengthy. Though some of its details are relevant to the moral question, it will suit my purpose best to begin with a broad sketch of the problem and to attend only to these details that seem relevant.

An important moral objection to the ND policy, perhaps the fundamental moral objection, can be expressed in the form of a simple argument.

> (M1) If it is morally justifiable to threaten to respond to a nuclear attack with nuclear retaliation then it is morally justifiable to use nuclear weapons under these conditions.
>
> But (M2) There are no conditions which would morally justify the use of nuclear weapons.
>
> Threfore, (M3) It is not morally justifiable to threaten to respond to a nuclear attack with nuclear retaliation.

Given that this tollendo argument is formally valid (or can be made so with minor alterations) I shall concentrate on the premisses and the conclusion. Though some defenders of the deterrence policy would reject either or both of the premisses, others might reject the whole argument as being irrelevant to the acceptability of that policy, though not of course to its moral acceptability. This could be the response of those who adopt a sort of 'moral nihilism with respect to nuclear deterrence' or, less radically, who regard no moral considerations as being of overriding importance to this sort of situation. I shall comment on these manoeuvres later in this paper, but my primary concern is with those who regard the nuclear deterrence policy as morally defensible, and who would therefore need to reject at least one of the premisses (M1) and (M2). Let us begin with those who accept (M2) but reject (M1). This would be the situation of those who believe that, given what we know of the nature of nuclear weapons, their actual use would indeed be monstrously immoral; but that the possession of such weapons as a deterrent to any would-be aggressor is justifiable, and arguably even a moral obligation upon those who cherish and wish to defend the values and ideals of western civilization.

The suggestion has sometimes been made that such plausibility that (M1) possesses derives from the assumption that (M1) is a particular application of the more general principle that *it is always wrong to threaten to do something which is itself wrong*. This principle they claim is false. I agree that it is indeed false, but it's important to see why.

Firstly, there is a well-known but commonly neglected distinction between two senses of the expression "morally wrong". It sometimes can mean 'morally objectionable', and at other times it is used in a stronger sense to mean 'morally unjustifiable'. An action or policy is wrong in the former sense if by virtue of its very nature it has some bad or undesirable feature which constitutes a moral reason why actions of that kind should not be performed. This situation obtains whenever a particular action of a certain kind requires justification, promise-breaking being an example. Promise-breaking is morally objectionable but it is obviously not necessarily morally unjustifiable, for in some circumstances the moral objections to it may be outweighed by reasons which require it. Moreover, when special circumstances do make a wrong action morally justifiable, the reasons which made it intrinsically morally objectionable don't suddenly cease to have any force. They are simply overriden by the reasons which justify it. So, in this way, it may not be wrong to threaten to do something which is itself wrong.

Secondly, even if an action were of such a kind that no circumstances could make it morally justifiable, it might still be morally justifiable to threaten to do it. This is because the threat to do x does not entail the conditional intention to do x, and is even compatible with the intention never to do x. The latter case, of course, involves deception, but unless one adopts the implausible moral stand that deception is not merely morally objectionable, but necessarily morally *unjustifiable*, there seems no reason to suppose that there couldn't be circumstances in which it would be morally justifiable to threaten to do x, even when x is itself an action which no circumstances could morally justify, *provided* that the agent making the threat had no intention of carrying it out.

In short, if the threatened action though itself morally objectionable (and in that sense wrong) is nevertheless morally justifiable in terms of some further consequential good, or if the threat does not involve forming the conditional intention to carry it out should it fail its purpose, then threatening to do x may be right even though doing x is wrong. Moreover these seem to be the only conditions in which this is true. What I want to argue is that neither of these conditions obtains in the actual international political scenario in which the nuclear threat finds its setting. That is, I shall argue that the deterrence policy does involve forming the conditional intention to use nuclear weapons in certain conditions, and that the fulfillment of that conditional intention under those conditions could not possibly be justified in terms of some further consequential good. Firstly then I shall try to show why the threat to retaliate (with nuclear weapons) necessarily does involve forming the conditional intention to use them (should the threat fail its purpose).

If a threat is going to be an effective means of influencing the actions of those to whom it is directed, it has to be credible. The only way, therefore, in which a threat can be accompanied by an intention never to carry it out, and at the same time effectively influence the behaviour of those to whom it is directed, is for that intention to be concealed. No one is influenced by threats which are *perceived* to be idle or insincere. Though politicians and statesmen are certainly skilled in the art of deception, I agree with those who have argued at length that the practical difficulties involved in a nation like the United States or the Soviet Union combining a credible policy of nuclear deterrence with the secret resolution never to implement that threat, are so great as to be virtually insuperable. Among those who have held the view that the deterrence policy *is* morally defensible, I am not aware of any who have argued that either of the nuclear super-powers can, in all circumstances, be relied upon to refrain from nuclear retaliation. I shall therefore not discuss this possibility further.

A more sophisticated move, however, is to argue that though on the international scene the credibility problem rules out the possibility of combining a threat to retaliate with the secret intention not to, it still does not follow that the threat to retaliate entails the conditional intention to carry it out. This is because it is possible to threaten to do x under certain circumstances without forming *any* intention, one way or the other, as to what one will do should those circumstances obtain. *Not* knowing whether an attack would result in massive retaliation may deter a potential nuclear aggressor just as effectively as knowing that it would. It would seem therefore that deterrence *can* be a credible policy without it being necessary to form the conditional intention to retaliate (which, of course, is not the same as forming the intention not to). This position is developed with some subtlety by Hare and Joynt[1] but I believe their argument fails. I shall try to show why.

The reason why threatening to do x is logically compatible with neither intending to do x nor intending not to is that there can be, and normally is, a significant time interval between the proclamation of a threat and its performance should it fail its purpose. Given that there are two separate intentional acts (viz. making the threat and carrying it out), not only is there, of course, no logical connection between these two acts, but also there may be sensible moral reasons for postponing forming the second intention at the time of forming the first. This is not just because, if the threat succeeds, carrying it out will not be necessary. Of more importance is that morally relevant facts may emerge in the intervening time-interval which were unforeseeable at the time of making the threat and which would render the performance of the threatened action morally unjustifiable, without however impugning the justifiability of making the threat in the first place.

But none of this is of any help in morally justifying the nuclear deterrence policy. The essential weakness of Hare and Joynt's argument is that it does not really face up to the problem that we have to decide *now* whether a nuclear attack would morally justify nuclear retaliation. There can be no question of waiting till the threat fails before deciding whether it is justifiable to implement it. I suspect that this is one of the ways in which we have not fully come to terms with the changes that the advent of nuclear weapons requires of our moral thinking. In the past, in political situations where issuing a threat has been appropriate and morally justifiable, it may well have been both feasible and morally desirable not to be committed to its implementation. This moral strategy is obviously not possible in the case of the ND policy since military technology necessitates that, should deterrence fail, retaliation be as near as possible to instantaneous. Unless it is, retaliation may not even be possible, and if it's not possible then the deterrence policy is no deterrent at all. But even if it *were* feasible to delay the forming of an intention to retaliate till and when it is known that the policy has failed, this would only be justifiable if it were reasonable to suppose that, in the event of a nuclear attack we might know *then*, what we do not know *now*, of some morally relevant facts which *would* justify nuclear retaliation after all. But to suppose this is of course to reject (M2) which says that there are *no* conditions which would morally justify the use of nuclear weapons.

It seems clear then that if (M2) is accepted then the claim that a threat does not necessarily involve having a conditional intention to act on it, though true, does not constitute a satisfactory reason for rejecting (M1). This is because in the case of the nuclear deterrence policy, the technical and political realities are such that any credible threat to retaliate necessarily does involve having the conditional intention to use nuclear weapons should that threat fail its purpose.

However, I claimed earlier that another way in which it is justifiable to threaten to do something morally wrong (even when the threat *does* involve a conditional intention) is when the threatened action is such that, though morally objectionable, nevertheless it would be morally justifiable in terms of the greater consequential good which its performance would achieve. To apply this to the nuclear deterrence policy amounts to denying (M2). So we must now ask, could there be circumstances which would morally justify the use of nuclear weapons?

Same people would unhesitatingly answer "yes" to this question and point to the circumstances of 1945 where nuclear weapons were in fact used quite justifiably, as they would claim. Others might argue that even if their use in that particular instance was morally dubious, there *could* be circumstances that would justify employing nuclear weapons. Bernard Williams, for example, claims that

> if a country were in fact faced with a clear, immediate and realistic intention by another aggressive power to destroy everybody in that country, for instance by nuclear means, then its government would be justified in using a nuclear attack to prevent it happening. In such a case, namely where at least one population or large set of persons is going to be destroyed anyway, and the other lot are the aggressors, a nuclear retaliation could be appropriate.[2]

Though Williams makes it clear in the chapter from which this passage is quoted that he believes such a situation *would* morally justify the use of nuclear weapons, what he doesn't make clear is *why* it would. In so far as he provides any reasons at all, they are presumably thought to be implied in his description of the imagined situation. Implicit seems to be the claim that in the context of international relations, if it's a case of them or us, and their aggressive intentions are clear and immediate, then it's morally justifiable that their population should be destroyed rather than ours. But this is surely to place an enormous moral weight on the principle that it's justifiable to kill in self-defence (always assuming that that is the principle Williams is implicitly appealing to). What is being neglected even in Williams' hypothetical example, and what never must be neglected in more realistic hypothetical situations, are the moral implications which flow from the sheer scale, and utterly indiscriminate nature, of the destructive power of nuclear weapons. In the light of these facts, the moral appeal to the principle of self-defence is a ludicrously inadequate basis on which to justify an act which would mean death or indescribable misery not only for the millions of innocent people who happen to belong to the nation whose leaders acted aggressively, but also for the millions more whose own nations may not have been politically involved at all. In short then, at least when the scope of (M2) is restricted to political scenarios which constitute realistic possibilities, (M2) seems hard to deny if moral considerations have any relevance at all.

This explains, I believe, why it has seemed obvious to many that the only way of defending the deterrence policy without sacrificing moral credibility is to reject (M1) and not (M2). But we have already seen that arguments typically deployed against (M1) turn out to be plausible only when (M2) is covertly rejected as well. Hence the case for the moral defensibility of deterrence begins to look extremely weak.

However, suppose we now look at the policy from the point of view of someone who is convinced that the deterrence policy is in fact succeeding in keeping the nuclear peace, and hence in avoiding the moral catastrophe that would indisputably occur should nuclear war break out. Such a person may be no less anxious to avoid a nuclear holocaust than any ban-the-bomb protester. But no amount of moral indignation (he will say) can disinvent the bomb. Given that it is with us, whether we like it or not, and that unscrupulous people or nations will certainly use it if they think that doing so will be to their advantage, we have to adopt realistic measures to *prevent* them from doing so. Moral sensitivity, such a person might plausibly claim, if combined with a steady refusal to face up to certain military and political realities, adds up to moral irresponsibility, not its opposite.

From this point of view, what appears persuasive is the ponendo argument which results from combining (M1) with the denial of (M3) to yield the conclusion that it is justifiable to use nuclear weapons *under certain conditions*, which of course is the denial of (M2). Call this argument (P):

(M1) If it is morally justifiable to threaten to respond to a nuclear attack with nuclear retaliation, then it is morally justifiable to use nuclear weapons under those conditions.

(P2) It is morally justifiable to threaten to respond to a nuclear attack with nuclear retaliation (the denial of (M3)).

therefore,

(P3) There are conditions which would morally justify the use of nuclear weapons (the denial of (M2)).

Though the acceptance of this argument involves grasping a very painful nettle indeed, the point of grasping a nettle firmly is precisely to avoid a much greater pain. Defenders of argument (P) therefore will insist that the pain of accepting (P3) has got to be measured against the considerable benefits which flow from the truth of (P2). They would claim that we need to take extremely seriously the fact that for nearly forty years the nuclear peace has been preserved, and they take it to be virtually self-evident that an important factor, perhaps the most important single factor, in accounting for this must be the efficacy of the deterrence policy – the policy of mutually assured destruction. If in fact it *does* work then, given that its morally laudable aim – the preservation of nuclear peace, and the mutual prevention of either of the superpowers imposing its political ideology on the other – its moral justifiability has surely got to be assessed in terms of its track record.

This pragmatic moral justification of the deterrence policy does of course involve a number of assumptions that are highly questionable and which indeed have often been questioned. For example, arguments that lean heavily on historical counterfactuals are notoriously difficult to defend, and moral deontologists will feel uneasy with the rather blatantly consequentialist nature of the moral reasoning. Moreover, the argument has to employ estimates of relevant probabilities which don't admit of accurate calculation and perhaps involve giving probability weightings to factors which are strictly incommensurable. However, though these difficulties are significant, and may even prove to be insurmountable, it is not my purpose to discuss them. Let's assume they could all be answered satisfactorily. We are still left with a major problem. For even on the assumption that the deterrence policy has worked, and on the even more dubious assumption that it will go on working, and that consequentialist utility-maximising moral reasoning is appropriate in this sort of context (which perhaps is reasonable enough), the pragmatic moral defence of the deterrence policy *still* has to face the central difficulty of justifying the use of nuclear weapons should the deterrent fail. How will it be possible to make use of utility-maximising moral reasoning to defend (P2) if the only context in which it would be justifiable to use nuclear weapons is the very context in which it is admitted that their use could not possibly do any good? We have already seen the futility of those attempts to get rid of this paradox by trying to drive a wedge between morally justifying the threat to retaliate and morally justifying carrying out that threat should it fail. Those who accept argument (P) at least recognise that (M1) and (P2) stand or fall together. Their problem however is that the very theory of moral reasoning which underlies their defence of (P2) would seem also to require them to reject (M1).

What I believe amounts to a serious and elaborate attempt to defend both (M1) and (P2) (argument (P)) has appeared recently in an article by David Gauthier.[3] In fairness it must be pointed out that his article is not primarily concerned with the *moral* justification of the deterrence policy at all but with its *rational* justification. However, a discussion of his argument is relevant to my purpose for two reasons. Firstly, having argued for the possibility that the deterrence policy is rationally justifiable he adds that, if it is, then it is also morally justifiable. Secondly, he operates with a concept of rationality spelt out in terms of agent-utility-maximisation. Though of course there is a fundamentally important difference between agent-utility-maximisation and the moral principle of general-utility-maximisation, this difference will not concern us when we consider Gauthier's argument for defending the two premisses which are the analogues of (M1) and (P2). What he tries to show is that it is possible that the deterrence policy is rationally justifiable, and that if it is then the implementation of the threat in the event of failure is *also* rationally justifiable *even though such implementation would admittedly do the agent no good*. Hence Gauthier faces the same task of getting rid of the paradox involved in asserting that an action which is admitted to be the opposite of utility-maximising can nevertheless be rational if it is required by a policy which is itself utility-maximising. His argument can be represented thus:

> (G1) If it is rationally justifiable to threaten to respond to a nuclear attack with nuclear retaliation, then it is rationally justifiable to use nuclear weapons under these conditions
>
> (G2) It is rationally justifiable ... etc.
>
> therefore
>
> (G3) It is rationally justifiable to respond to nuclear attack with nuclear retaliation.

Fundamentally, Gauthier argues that the justifiability of the deterrence policy depends on "balancing the benefits of deterrent success against costs of deterrent failure" (p. 455) and that the calculation of these costs and benefits must take into account the relevant probabilities of being in the undesirable situation both with and without the policy. Hence he is careful not to claim that the ND policy is *necessarily* utility-maximising. He concedes that whether it is or not may be extraordinarily difficult to determine. However, what he does insist on is that such a policy is not necessarily irrational either, and that in particular it cannot be shown to be such simply on the grounds that carrying out the deterrent intention (in the event of policy failure) would itself not be utility-maximising. For though responding to nuclear attack with massive nuclear retaliation certainly is irrational when considered in abstraction from the deterrence policy, if having the policy is itself utility-maximising, then even if deterrence fails, acting on the conditional intention to retaliate will also be rational, since it partakes of the rationality of the policy as a whole. In a word, his point is that whether or not retaliation is rational depends on whether or not the deterrence policy (of which it is a part) is rational. To put the point another way, unleashing nuclear weapons when viewed under the description of retaliation could be rational, even though this same performance would be irrational under any other description.

Essential to Gauthier's argument is his insistence on the need to recognise that in balancing the benefits of deterrent success against the costs of deterrent failure, each expectation must be probability-weighted. Thus, if a relatively high probability of deterrent success depends on a genuine willingness to carry out the threat in the event of deterrent failure, then the expected gain from deterrence could exceed the expected cost of failure, even if failure when abstracted from its probability-weighting would involve costs which are virtually infinite. But the rational advocate of the deterrence policy calculates that *just because* the costs of deterrent failure when considered in abstraction are so unacceptably high for *everyone*, this ensures that deterrent failure will have a low probability. This in turn enables probability-weighted benefits of success to exceed probability-weighted costs of failure.

I believe that Gauthier's theory has the considerable merit of recognising that the rational assessment of retaliation (should the need for that action arise) is inseparable from the rational assessment of the deterrence policy as a whole. No attempt is made to drive a wedge between the justification of *adopting* the deterrence policy and the justification of *acting* on it should deterrence fail. The justification of one stands or falls with the justification of the other. Gauthier seems to think that this is true of deterrence policies in general but, even if that is doubtful, it is surely true in the case of the nuclear deterrence policy. If one accepts this policy as justifiable then (as we have already seen) there can be no question of being able to review the justifiabity of acting on it if and when deterrence fails. On Gauthier's view then there is no escape from the conclusion that if the probability-weighted nett benefits of adopting the deterrence policy exceed the probability-weighted nett benefits of any alternative non-deterrence policy (and it seems clear that he believes this to be so) then in the relatively unlikely event of deterrence failure, it would still be both rationally and morally justifiable to retaliate, even though such retaliation would admittedly bring about the ultimate apocalyptic horror. In that awful event, those few who push the buttons to send the missiles on their retaliatory mission, together with the hundreds of thousands whose training, expertise and co-operation made it all technically possible, together with the millions who have given the deterrence policy their moral and political support, together with the hundreds of millions who have not registered any opposition to that policy – all these people (if he is right) will have the satisfaction of knowing that at least the act of ending civilization with such a *bang*, and with so *many* whimpers, was both rationally and morally justified, since after all it was an integral part of a rationally and morally justifiable policy.

I suppose it is obvious that I regard Gauthier's argument as a reductio, but given that it was not *intended* as such, we must try to locate just where things have gone wrong.

"Probability," said Bishop Butler (with uncharacteristic exaggeration), "is the very guide of life". It is certainly true that practical reasoning, including much of our moral reasoning, is not possible without involving probability judgments. But it is important to see clearly just how estimates of probabilities enter into our practical reasoning. Suppose we are not sure whether it would be justifiable to do some action x. Our doubts could arise in two different ways. On the one hand we may be in no doubt that if the facts are as we believe them to be, then doing x would certainly not be justifiable. In this case our doubts relate to whether indeed we have got our facts right. On the other hand we may know very well what the relevant facts are, but nevertheless be unsure how much moral weight to attach to them. In this case our doubts are not a function of the gaps in our empirical knowledge. They relate to uncertainty about more subtle and elusive questions. How should we order our moral priorities? What ideals should we adopt? What sort of person do we want to be? It is important to notice that of these two distinguishable ways in which doubts enter into our practical thinking, judgements of probability relate to the first but not to the second.

Now concerning the question of whether the deterrence policy is justifiable we can indeed raise the question of how probable it is that the policy will succeed in deterring. But this probability is not relevant to the question of whether, *if it fails*, it would be justifiable to *act* on the policy, for the facts relating to the justifiability of *that* act are not in serious doubt. In so far as we already know now that a situation of deterrence failure would be a situation of unprecedented and unimaginable disaster, then given that we also know *now* that retaliation would result in further disaster enormously compounded, we know *now* that such retaliation could not possibly be morally justifiable. Expressed generally, the probability of our ever being in a situation in which we are faced with the decision whether or not to do x is irrelevant to whether it would be justifiable to do x, so long as we already know *now* what we would need to know *then* if we had to decide whether such an act was justifiable.

But, it might be replied, suppose we could be certain that the ND policy would not fail, and that retaliation would therefore never be necessary. Wouldn't this amply justify that policy since, ex hypothesi, it would succeed in keeping the nuclear peace? And if this point is conceded, then what about an extremely high probability of success? If it is admitted that a success probability of 1 is relevant to the question of whether the conditional intention to retaliate is justifiable, how can a probability of .99 not be relevant?

This argument is certainly seductive. Bernard Williams is probably not the only philosopher of note who has embraced it, or at least flirted with it.[4] It is nevertheless fallacious. The fallacy lies in not noticing that if it is believed to be *certain* that the deterrence policy will succeed in its purpose, then no clear sense can be attached to the notion that the policy involves a conditional intention to retaliate. Intending to do x entails believing it possible to do x. If we believe it certain that the conditions requiring retaliation will *never* obtain, then it is not possible to *intend* to retaliate under those conditions. But since my criticism of the deterrence policy has been based on the already defended claim that if it is not possible to justify retaliation it is not possible to justify the conditional intention to retaliate, then obviously my argument has no application to situations where the question of justifying retaliation does not even arise.

However, situations in which that question does arise are precisely those in which the possibility of deterrence failure arises, *however remote that possibility might be*. Once the possibility is admitted, then given the momentous consequences which hang upon our answer, we have to face now the question whether acting on the conditional intention to retaliate would be justifiable. The only bearing that the probability of deterrence failure can have on *that* question concerns the degree of urgency with which the question claims our attention. And, of course, the probability of failure is not the only factor which determines that degree of urgency.

The primary purpose of this paper has been to defend argument (M). At the beginning, I mentioned that some might accept that argument as sound, but reject it as irrelevant to the ND policy on the grounds that morality is irrelevant to nuclear politics, either because it has no application at all in such contexts, or else because other considerations are of overriding importance. On these views I shall make only the following brief observations.

If morality has to do with anything, it has to do with reasons for acting, or refraining from acting, when the well-being of sentient beings is at stake. It would be strange indeed if morality had application when those whose interests are affected are relatively small in number, and no application when such numbers are counted in hundreds of millions. Moreover, what considerations could be of *more* importance than matters of life and death, happiness and misery, civilized living or barbarism – matters which constitute the very substance of what moral questions are about? I suspect that when morality is rejected as irrelevant to such issues as nuclear war and nuclear policies people have in mind a conception of the moral life which deals in the currency of clean hands and pure hearts and which travels the high moralistic road that dispenses with having to bother with the facts. I hope it has been clear that no such conception of morality underlies the arguments of this paper. I have been at some pains to point out that attempts to defend the ND policy as morally justifable typically come to grief precisely because political realities and relevant technological facts are either ignored or not taken seriously.

For all that, it is certainly reasonable to ask what is the moral alternative to nuclear deterrence. Though multilateral nuclear disarmament is clearly desirable, nobody seems to know how it can be achieved. The only remaining alternative seems to be unilateral disarmament and appeasement. It is just because this last seems so obviously unacceptable to many that they have concluded that the policy of deterrence is the option which is the least evil.

I doubt whether these simple alternatives *are* the only practical options available, but even if they are not, it is hardly likely that rejecting deterrence would be without cost. We are already too far down the nuclear track to be able to turn back without great risks, and perhaps terrible suffering. We have for too long ignored the radical changes that the advent of nuclear weapons demands of our moral and political thinking. We may have to give up some of our cherished freedoms – freedoms for which earlier generations were prepared to sacrifice their lives. Governments may have to forego much of their political autonomy. The nation-state may have to go the way of the feudal system. After all, political structures, even if they last for a few hundred years (which most of them don't) are relatively transitory phenomena. I don't deny that the rejection of deterrence might make life grim, and demand great sacrifice. But even if it does involve suffering and the disappearance, at least for a time, of opportunities to exercise our cherished freedoms and the pursuit of our most valued ideals, it does not demand the sacrifice of those ideals themselves. What I have tried to show in this paper, however, is that *to accept the deterrence policy is already to have given up those ideals*. It is to endorse a policy which necessarily involves being ready now, should circumstances demand it, to unleash forces whose evil effects would be literally mind-boggling and which would, it is freely admitted, be unredeemed by any consequential good. To be thoroughly prepared to do this, however unlikely we think it might be necessary, is surely already to have abandoned every moral ideal of freedom, justice, compassion and goodness to which civilized human beings have aspired. But to be thoroughly prepared to do this precisely in order to preserve and *defend* those ideals can be nothing less than the ultimate in moral absurdity.

Notes

1. See J. E. Hare and Carey B. Joynt, *Ethics and International Affairs* (Macmillan, London, 1982).
2. Bernard Williams, 'Morality, scepticism and the nuclear arms race', in *Objections to Nuclear Defence*, ed. N. Blake and K. Pole (Routledge and Kegan Paul, London, 1984), p. 105.
3. D. Gauthier, 'Deterrence, maximisation and rationality', *Ethics*, April 1984.
4. Williams, op. cit.

Postscript

The international situation which prompted the writing of this paper was when the 'cold war' of the 1980s had reached its height. The tension which had arisen between Russia in the East and the USA, Britain and France in the West can scarcely be imagined by those who were not alive at the time. All of these nations were armed with nuclear weapons in such numbers and of such destructive power that if even only a few were used virtually all life on the planet would be destroyed, except perhaps for some insect species plus some even more primitive organisms. Moreover, these weapons were capable of being released within minutes of receiving orders from these nations' leaders. They could be launched from numerous land bases in America, Europe and the Soviet Union or from submarines scattered throughout the world's oceans. This meant that an accidental release of a nuclear weapon arising from some human or mechanical error on either side would trigger a massive retaliation from the targeted nation. Some experts regarded the likelihood of this occurring as so high that, sooner or later, disaster was almost inevitable in view of the large number of opportunities for a mistake to occur. Ironically, the policy of nuclear deterrence was widely believed in the West to be necessary to protect the ideals of freedom and democracy, and in the Soviet Union principally as a defence of communism from potential aggression from America and its allies.

It so happened that, also in the nineteen eighties, at Canterbury University there was a concern among some academics that the scholarly contributions from those who held the rank of professor were not necessarily more significant than these from non-professors. Consequently, an ad hoc committee comprising both elected professors and non-professors was set up to examine the particular role and relative importance of professors in the university. I was elected to the committee as one of the lecturers' representatives.

The committee met a number of times, and each meeting lasted a considerable time. At one such meeting, when the discussion had sunk to a particularly boring level, I looked around at those attending. I noted that among the academic disciplines represented, were scholars from both the physical and biological sciences, computer science, engineering, history, English, psychology, political science, sociology, philosophy, modern languages (including Russian) and some others. Any solution to the highly complex problem facing the world constituted by the nuclear predicament would surely benefit from contributions from experts in all these disciplines. Shouldn't this be the topic of our discussion rather than the one we were discussing?

Subsequently, therefore, I sent an invitation to all members of the academic staff to attend a weekend at the university field station at Cass specifically in order to discuss this topic. Quite a good number of my colleagues responded positively, and the weekend seminar was reasonably well attended. To serve as a starting point for discussion, I read a paper on the morality of nuclear deterrence. The foregoing, a revised version of this paper, was later published in a special issue of *Critical Philosophy* (vol. 3, 1986), which was entirely devoted to philosophical papers on nuclear armaments.

10
Review of *Practical Medical Ethics*

[*Bioethics*, vol; 7 no.1, Jan. 1993]

All the authors of this useful book (*Practical Medical Ethics*, by Alistair Campbell, Grant Gillett and Gareth Jones, Oxford University Press, 1992) have professional expertise in medicine and two in the field of philosophical ethics. They have all published extensively in bioethics and hold senior positions in the Medical School of the University of Otago. Not surprisingly, they make a splendid team and have produced a short manual which has a remarkable unity of style and purpose often lacking in multi-author volumes. They speak with a single voice, and though their argument is not entirely free of inconsistencies, these are fewer than are found in many single-author works.

In their preface, the authors state that their book is addressed specifically to medical students and medical practitioners rather than to health professionals generally (hence the somewhat less than trendy title); but as they explain, this is not because they believe that 'medical ethics is only for doctors', but because they did not want to skim over some of the harder moral issues which more specifically face medical practitioners. Nevertheless, they express the hope that the book will reach an audience that goes beyond the confines of the medical profession. Given that it is relatively free of medical jargon, eminently readable, and characterised throughout by a balanced, warm and humane approach to its subject matter, their hope deserves to be realised.

They begin with a brief sketch of the philosophical foundations of medical ethics (on which more in a moment) followed by a splendid chapter on the "healing ethos" in which the authors sensitively explore what they regard as the ethical foundations of good medical practice. (Given the direction of change towards a market-driven system of health care characterising the New Zealand scene at the present time, one can only hope that the current generation of medical students will not only read, mark, learn and inwardly digest, but also vigorously strive to preserve the principles and attitudes so eloquently expressed in this chapter.) The remaining sections deal with a wide range of ethical issues including the use of cadavers in teaching and research, organ transplants, foetal research, abortion, neonatal and childhood issues, euthanasia and suicide. One chapter is devoted to the special ethical dilemmas that arise in connection with psychiatric medicine and another is devoted to those surrounding the topic of AIDS. There is a timely discussion on medicine and society dealing with questions of justice in the funding and rationing of society's resources for healthcare, and the final chapter explores the related issues of professional ethics, etiquette and malpractice. Throughout, judicious use is made of brief case histories which invariably help to clarify the relevance of the ethical principles appealed to in the authors' discussions, and at the same time fully justify the inclusion of "practical" in the book's title. The book concludes with three appendices dealing with codes of ethics, biculturalism, and issues in genetics. There is an index and a useful bibliography.

Given that the authors are primarily addressing medical students and medical practitioners, it might seem churlish to have any complaints about the opening chapter. Admittedly, it is difficult to provide a satisfactory introduction to the philosophical foundations of medical ethics in a short book which is not intended to make a contribution to philosophy or even aimed at readers who can be assumed to have an amateur interest in that subject. Yet, because "medical ethics is an applied branch of ethics or moral philosophy" (p. 1), such an introduction can hardly be omitted altogether, since, aware of them or not, readers will inevitably bring to the subject their own philosophical presuppositions. Since these are often little better than prejudices, some attempt at laying them bare and if possible subjecting them to critical rational scrutiny would seem to be desirable. However, readers innocent of any background in moral philosophy are likely to have some of their prejudices reinforced rather than exposed by this chapter. For example, the exposition and criticism of utilitarianism, arguably the most thoroughly developed and widely discussed of any theory of normative ethics, is ludicrously inadequate. It is distressing to see these authors fall into the common trap of expounding a grotesquely oversimplified version of this theory and then 'refuting' it by means of one or two intuitively based counter-examples. (A reference to Elizabeth Anscombe's remark to the effect that to take seriously the logical implications of utilitarianism is evidence of "a corrupt mind" is thrown in for good measure.) This sort of approach is regrettable, since the authors are very far from endorsing simple-minded intuitionism, and nor do they accept a version of 'virtue ethics' favoured by those who think that medical ethics can simply be based on the opinions and judgment of healthcare workers of integrity. What they seek is "an independent conception of what it is for professionals to act rightly in their clinical lives."(p. 7) Yet, having decisively rejected utilitarianism, it is both ironical and fascinating to see them persuasively providing rational support for the familiar principles of autonomy, beneficence, confidentiality, informed consent, justice, etc. by drawing attention to the consequences for human well-being of their acceptance. Also, they are well aware that ethical dilemmas arise precisely in those situations where such principles come into conflict with one another, and since they see none of them as having any absolute status, they recognise the need for some rational means of resolving such conflicts. Again and again their way of doing so is by paying close attention to all the morally relevant features of the particular circumstances and choosing that action which would seem, in the long run, to have the best consequences for all whose interests are likely to be affected. All this seems sensible and rational – and in the best utilitarian tradition!

Unfortunately, rationality is much less in evidence when euthanasia is discussed. The authors believe that it is wrong to prolong a person's life when doing so could not substantially benefit the patient (passive euthanasia) but, in line with a deeply entrenched medical tradition, actively ending patients' lives at their request is firmly rejected, even when it is clear that allowing life to continue would also "not substantially benefit the patient". Now the authors are aware that "most philosophers do not recognise a moral difference between acts and omissions" (p. 115) *in those circumstances in which the foreseeable outcome is identical* (the crucially important italicised qualification is unfortunately omitted), and they quote a well known argument from James Rachels, a defender of this view. They agree that "[the morally relevant] difference between killing and letting die cannot rest on whether or not one performs certain active bodily movements" (p. 115) and state that "we have to look further for the reasons for believing in a [morally relevant] difference". They continue: "The British Medical Association gave a number of such reasons" (in *Euthanasia*, 1988) and they then quote four statements from that report. What is astonishing is that not one of the quoted "reasons" addresses the issue of the active/passive distinction at all. All four are simply reasons submitted for rejecting active euthanasia. But if the moral relevance of the acts/omissions distinction cannot be sustained, any arguments for rejecting active euthanasia are also arguments for rejecting passive euthanasia. It is therefore of crucial importance for the traditional view that the intuition that there is a moral difference between active and passive euthanasia be clearly shown to have a firm foundation and is not simply an irrational prejudice. The philosophical case for the conclusion that it is just that may of course be mistaken, but if it is, the arguments in this book fall a long way short of showing it.

Postscript

My criticism of the authors' inadequate treatment of the question whether there is an ethically relevant distinction between killing and letting die is expanded in the next two papers. A thorough discussion of this question (when set against a background of carefully qualified conditions) in my opinion is urgently needed whenever consideration is given to legal changes relating to euthanasia and medically assisted suicide. The first paper is my submission to the 2016 Parliamentary Select Committee on the subject. (However, my views on this question have not changed substantially for many decades.) The second paper, published in 1999, is an attack on Grant Gillett's defence of the official and traditional attitude of the medical profession on the matter. Grant told me that his essay was the text of a talk which he gave to a meeting of medical professionals, and that it was "very well received". Concerning complex ethical questions, what alarmed me was Grant's "post-modernist" approach. In essence, this approach is sympathetic to the view that respect for logical rigour in philosophical argument is just a personal option and no better than, and not even as good as, reliance on moral intuitions which arise out of medical experience.

11
Killing and letting die: a morally relevant distinction?

The sad case of Lecretia Seales is a reminder that it is increasingly obvious that the euthanasia debate will not go away. What is not so obvious is why it won't. I suspect that part of the reason is because politicians see the morality of euthanasia as involving a fundamental division in moral public opinion. In a democracy, responsible legislators try to make laws which as far as possible reflect what they take to be the moral values of the general public. There is now no doubt that a significant proportion of the public believe that an individual's choice not to go on living should be respected. On the other hand, traditional medical opinion is firmly opposed to euthanasia. It is seen as being diametrically opposed to the conviction that a doctor's fundamental duty is to respect and save life, a point of view aften reinforced by religious belief and expressed in terms of the Sanctity of Life principle. (This is not to say that all who accept that principle are necessarily religious believers.)

In short, sincere advocates of voluntary euthanasia can be said to be appealing to the principle of respect for persons, an essential ingredient of which is the paramount importance of an individual's capacity to have control over what happens to their own body. On the other hand those who firmly reject euthanasia are equally convinced that to allow doctors to become "killers" goes against the ancient medical obligation to preserve life, and would also inevitably lead to an erosion of trust in doctors. It might also provide an opportunity for emotional blackmail on the part of unscrupulous relatives and others who desire to be relieved of the burden of care of the terminally ill. No wonder politicians see the task of reconciling these mutually opposing but morally laudable convictions as being beyond the capacity of the legislators to resolve.

What is less obvious, and all too seldom discussed, is that the law already enshrines what has every appearance of being a contradiction, or at least a paradoxical tension of principles, which cries out for urgent resolution.

Within the medical fraternity there is a widely accepted ethical principle that an individual should have the 'power of veto' when it comes to medical intervention of their own body. This has the full backing of the law, especially since the Cartwright Report and the subsequent formation of the Code of Patient's Rights. Patients should not suffer medical intervention without their informed consent. This means that if patients clearly indicate their wish to be allowed to die through the withholding or withdrawing of all life-prolonging medical intervention, it would be unethical to continue to treat them. It would also be illegal. Note that this applies even in those situations where, in the opinion of expert medical opinion, withdrawing or withholding treatment would certainly result in a patient's imminent death.

On the other hand, even if a fully competent patient has clearly expressed a wish for their life to be ended, active killing of a patient is regarded by the medical establishment as certainly unethical. In the eyes of the law it amounts to criminal homicide.

Underlying this apparent contradiction is the assumption that there is both a moral and legal distinction to be made between active killing and allowing to die, *even in those circumstances where the result for the patient is virtually identical.* In my view, the most urgent need for progress in resolving disputes on the rights and wrongs of euthanasia is for an informed, rational discussion on whether or not the distinction between killing and letting die is indeed ethically relevant in these circumstances. Yet whenever I have heard politicians debating euthanasia when the subject has been before the House, I can't remember this question even being mentioned, let alone discussed.

It's important to recognise that "allowing to die" and "killing" do not mean the same thing. It's one thing to kill someone. It's quite another thing to allow someone to die. However, circumstances can never be neglected when considering the rights and wrongs of actions. Active killing requires a positive intentional act. Similarly, for an agent to allow someone to die is an intentional negative act *in those circumstances in which there is both the opportunity and the ability to save that person's life*. A negative act of this sort is sometimes described as "refraining from preventing death" or "an act of forbearance". Everyone recognises that in some circumstances we rightly hold people morally responsible for acts of forbearance. In particular, if a doctor was present at the scene of an accident where a person had received a life-threatening injury, the doctor would normally be held both morally and legally responsible if they failed to try to save the person's life. This is because we take it for granted that the accident victim almost certainly doesn't want to die. But if patients in a hospital have a cardiac arrest, and they have left clear instructions that in the event of a cardiac arrest they do not want to be resuscitated, then it is also recognised that there is an obligation on the medical staff not to prolong their life by this means. A patient's wishes have to be respected and are overriding in these circumstances.

On the face of it then, there is a good case for believing that in *some carefully qualified circumstances*, there is no ethically relevant distinction to be drawn between actively ending a person's life and intentionally allowing that person to die. The circumstances would include clear evidence that the person was of sound mind, and had, over a period of time, rationally considered and accepted the consequences of ending their life. If it is not merely justifiable but morally obligatory to obey patients' wishes for all life-preserving treatment to cease, even when they clearly understand that this would result in imminent death, then it would seem to be equally justifiable for their wishes to be followed if in the same circumstances they were to request that their life be ended, perhaps by a lethal injection of a high dose of morphine. Arguably, this procedure would be ethically far preferable in so far as it would normally involve much less suffering.

I have outlined a prima facie case for the view that in a carefully qualified context of medical care there is no ethically relevant difference between, on the one hand, actively killing patients in response to their rational and measured request and, on the other, allowing patients to die from the effects of the withdrawal of life-preserving treatment in response to their similarly qualified request. If the latter is not merely justifiable, but indeed both morally and legally obligatory, then so is the former. Whether this argument is convincing or not is a matter of controversy among professional ethicists. What is beyond question is its central importance to any informed, rational discussion of euthanasia and the related topic of assisted suicide. If the argument is flawed it needs to be shown to be so.

It would be a serious mistake to assume that this is all that there is to the rights and wrongs of euthanasia, for it is certainly an ethical and legal issue of considerable complexity. Outlining even some of its ramifications would require a paper of much greater length. I have confined my discussion simply to the one centrally important question to which all the other issues are arguably of peripheral significance. Yet it is discussion of this question that has suffered the most neglect both by politicians and by the general public at large. There is work to be done.

One final point. The Sanctity of Life principle is sometimes invoked in defense of the view that assisted suicide (which, in some circumstances, is a special case of voluntary euthanasia) is ethically unacceptable. Yet this principle is seldom held to be an absolute one, since it is widely regarded as being justifiably overridden in circumstances such as war, and killing in self-defence. Of course whether it is justifiably overridden in the case of voluntary euthanasia is another matter. But why is the Sanctity of Life principle held to be so important? Surely because if you deprive persons of their lives, you deprive them of everything that makes life worth living. Being alive is obviously a necessary condition for enjoying life. However, it's clearly not a sufficient condition. If, in the considered opinion of a competent individual, the prospect of continuing to live is completely bereft of enjoyment and offers nothing but increasing misery, suffering, and loss of human dignity, what is so sacred about life in these circumstances? There may be a good answer but it doesn't readily spring to mind.

Note

This paper was submitted to the Select Committee of Parliament considering proposed legislation on euthanasia and assisted suicide in January, 2016.

12

'Killing, Letting Die and Moral Perception': a reply to Grant Gillett

[*Bioethics*, vol. 13 no.5, October 1999]

One reason why health professionals, as well as the community at large, are so divided over the ethics of euthanasia is related to the centrally important question of whether there is a significant and ethically relevant distinction between killing and letting die. It has frequently been argued that unless this distinction is indeed ethically relevant, it is inconsistent to condemn active voluntary euthanasia but approve of respecting a patient's wishes to be allowed to die. If each of these options has the same outcome, then they are on the same ethical footing – they are both wrong or both ethically permissible.

Setting aside for the moment the difficulties involved in stating with any precision just what the killing/letting die distinction amounts to, it seems fair to say that whereas the ordinary citizen tends to find its ethical relevance somewhat obscure and elusive in those circumstances where the expected outcome is virtually identical, the medical professional who has been reared in the Hippocratic tradition is likely to regard it as having crucial significance. It is seen as separating the doctor's fundamental ethical duty never to go on treating a patient against that patient's wishes from the equally fundamental duty to preserve life and not to kill. On this issue, contemporary philosophers (with some significant exceptions) have tended to side with the ordinary citizen, but of course the doctors' viewpoint enjoys the support of the law.

Considered reflections on this topic by Grant Gillett, who is both a philosopher and a neurosurgeon, are therefore to be welcomed and deserve close attention.[1] What is of particular interest in Gillett's discussion is that although he basically defends the traditional medical stance on this issue, he draws back from endorsing an absolutist position. Both at the beginning of his article, as well as at the very end, he concedes that actively killing a patient "may, on occasion, be the only right thing to do".[2] However, he leaves us in no doubt that he believes such occasions would be extremely rare, and that even when such killings are morally justifiable, he regards it as entirely appropriate that "a doctor who intervenes to end her patient's life should do so knowing that the law disapproves of this act and that she might be called to close account for performing it".[3] Given that he also makes it clear that he believes "it is generally right to withdraw life-prolonging therapy when certain conditions are met", and that it is not merely morally permissible but morally obligatory to discontinue treating a patient if there is no doubt that that is their wish, the question whether there is indeed a morally relevant difference between killing and letting die is for Gillett one of crucial importance.[4]

Now, as it stands, the law allows no room for the exceptional circumstances which Gillett concedes may sometimes obtain. Supposing for a moment that his ethical stance on these matters (which might fairly be described as a carefully qualified conservatism) is correct, should the law be changed to reflect this? Perhaps not, for the relation between morality and the law is a complex one, and it is not always either practicable or desirable that what is ethically right or wrong should also respectively be legal or illegal. Gillett is certainly right to point out that it is neither inconsistent nor hypocritical to believe that killing a patient should continue to be against the law even though this action may on occasion be the right thing to do.

Nevertheless, whether the present situation with regard to the law is indeed ethically desirable is another matter. There seems little doubt that many doctors occasionally find themselves in circumstances where they are as certain as it is possible for any doctor to be about any medical decision that actively terminating the life of their patient at their patient's request is the morally right thing to do, but who refrain from doing it out of fear of criminal prosecution. On the other hand, if their patient were simply to ask that all life-sustaining treatment be withdrawn so that they may be allowed to die, not only does the law permit doctors to do this but it also *requires* them to do it, for it expressly forbids doctors to treat patients against their wishes. In other words, the law reinforces the traditional medical view that it is unethical to *ignore* the patient's wishes to be allowed to die, and also unethical to *accede* to the patient's wishes to be helped to die. In short, the law regards the distinction between killing and letting die as having pivotal moral significance. If therefore the law is to remain as it is, the assumed ethical relevance of this distinction needs to be made transparently clear, or else the law could prove to be a force which, in some circumstances, actually deters some conscientious doctors from doing what they believe is morally right.

Unfortunately, Gillett's aim seems to have been not so much to demonstrate clearly the moral relevance of the distinction in question, but rather to raise doubts concerning the arguments of those who have argued against its moral relevance. Of course, even if he were successful in this more modest enterprise this would not necessarily render the moral relevance of the distinction perspicuous, which I have argued is what is required. But, as it happens, he does not even succeed in the more limited task which he has set himself, as I shall try to show. Moreover, the reasons for his failure are highly instructive.

Gillett is aware that there have been a number of carefully argued attacks on the moral relevance of the killing/letting die distinction by contemporary philosophers but he avoids subjecting any of these arguments to extended critical analysis. Rather his strategy is to suggest that "general and abstract arguments fail to take account of the complex and particular situations which are found in the care of those with terminal illness. When in such situations, there are perceptions and intuitions available that do not easily find propositional form but lead most of those whose practice is in the care of the dying to resist active euthanasia."

In several passages he contrasts what he calls "the argument from moral perception", available to the clinicians and those who have the care of the dying and terminally ill, with "philosophical" reasons or arguments, and he pejoratively describes the latter as "clear or clear-cut, cogent, propositional, formalised, logical and sterile".

What could it mean to say that there is an "argument from moral perception" which is available to those who have the care of the dying and the terminally ill (but presumably not to those philosophers who don't)? In particular, does it mean that this argument cannot even be understood by the latter group, or simply that only the former group will be able to 'intuit' its soundness and relevance? Notoriously, appeals to moral intuitions which are available to some but not to others have an unfortunate tendency to be at best arbitrary and at worst arrogant and disempowering. This is not to deny that there is a legitimate role for the notion of moral intuition in ethical judgment. It is certainly true that making a responsible moral decision in any particular situation requires a sensitivity to what is morally relevant in that situation, a sensitivity to various subtle features which are often not easily captured in words, or even consciously present to the mind of the moral decision-maker. Decisions which are literally matters of life and death, made by clinicians and others who care for the terminally ill, will typically be of this kind. It is also true that when making such decisions, it is rarely if ever the case that the agent either consciously or unconsciously rehearses in their mind logical reasons or arguments in support of their decision. They can often appropriately be said to 'intuit' what they should do, and the more experienced and morally perceptive they are, the more appropriate will this expression be. All this is familiar to students of the phenomenology of ethical decision-making.

However, it is important not to confuse the phenomenology of particular instances of ethical decision-making with the rational justification of those decisions. The reason why 'intuitive' ethical decisions in particular situations often deserve to be taken seriously, especially when made by experienced, sensitive and morally perceptive agents, is that good reasons and arguments can be produced in support of those decisions, though not necessarily by the agents who made them. Intuitive ethical judgments have to earn their right to be taken seriously. If there is no way in which such intuitions can be given rational support, there is no way in which we can distinguish sound intuitions from judgments founded on ignorance and prejudice. Of course, what counts as 'rational support' is itself a complex issue and not free from controversy, but it certainly involves the deployment of reason and argument, and the clearer and more cogent the argument the better.

Furthermore, Gillett's appeal to the moral intuitions of a select group is notoriously open to the obvious difficulty which arises when some members of that same group declare that they have the opposite intuition. Given that a significant minority of those who care for the terminally ill sincerely believe that the distinction in question is not morally relevant, what are we to say of their intuitions? That they are morally blind? Without the support of reasons, therefore, it is hard to see how employing an 'argument from moral perception' on the basis of some sort of privileged intuition could show those who don't share that intuition that there is indeed an ethical relevance in the distinction between killing and letting die. Certainly such an 'argument' could not even begin to show that there is a weakness, or something lacking, in the philosophical arguments of those who have denied the moral relevance of the distinction, let alone that the attempt to render those arguments clear and cogent is somehow misguided or misconceived. This is simply because an assertion on the basis of a privileged, unexpressed intuition is not an argument at all, and nor does it suddenly and mysteriously become one by being dubbed "the argument from moral perception". In the absence of a conclusion based on at least one premiss there is no argument. To argue on the basis of an intuition for the conclusion that there is indeed an ethically relevant distinction between killing and letting die, the alleged intuition which constitutes the premiss must of course be distinct from the conclusion. Therefore, unless and until that intuition is given verbal expression and does not simply amount to a restatement of the conclusion it is supposed to support, there is no argument but simply bare assertion.

However, in the context of his discussion of intuition and moral perception Gillett makes two claims which, when properly understood, are certainly true and worth noting, viz.:

> a) patients' attitudes "do not lose their force in relation to a life and death decision just because they cannot be defended by rational arguments"; and
> b) "patients' overt requests are often an unreliable guide to their true wishes."[5]

Here Gillett makes two important and opposite points: that the words of dying patients cannot always be taken at face value, and that the words of dying patients must (often? always?) be taken seriously, even if the patients are not able to defend their decisions or wishes with rational arguments. Unfortunately, even if we are careful to express these points so as not to make them appear mutually contradictory, neither has the slightest relevance to the question at issue. This is because the words of dying patients sometimes express a wish to be allowed to die and sometimes a wish to be helped to die. What we would need if Gillett's points are to be relevant to his discussion are reasons for believing that in those situations where a patient expresses a wish to be allowed to die their words should be taken at face value (even if they are unable to defend their decision with rational arguments), but when patients express a wish to be helped to die, we should not take their words at face value, even if they are able to defend their decisions with rational arguments. It is not surprising that no reasons are given in support of this wildly implausible and arbitrary stance.

As a non-clinician, what I suspect is true is that the words of terminally ill patients should sometimes be taken at face value and sometimes not; that such patients are sometimes able to defend their decisions with rational arguments and sometimes not. In any case, it is certainly true that dying patients' attitudes always deserve to be respected, whether or not they can be defended by rational arguments. But clearly none of these truths, or truisms, has any bearing on the question at issue, namely whether there is indeed an ethically relevant distinction between killing and letting die.

The repeated appeal to intuition together with the strictures against clear and logical reasoning, both of which pervade Gillett's article, appear to have prevented him from noticing how frequently he tends to beg the question at issue. For example, when he quotes with approval Kubler-Ross's observation that "it is . . . not enough to listen only to the overt verbal communications of our patients", he is thinking of cases where the patient has asked for active euthanasia.[6] But since the quoted remark equally applies to requests from patients to be allowed to die it is hard to see how this could even seem to be relevant to the point at issue unless one had already assumed that there is indeed an ethically relevant difference between killing and letting die.

Similarly, Gillett makes considerable use of quotations from authors like Nussbaum, Wittgenstein and Aristotle to draw attention either to the mystery of death and the dying process or to the subtleties and difficulties associated with moral decision-making and the various (largely unsuccessful) attempts that have been made to give them clear, rational expression in the form of denumerable moral propositions. Some at least of these quotations encapsulate perceptive observations and serve as important correctives to any philosopher who may be insensitive to the complexity of the moral issues surrounding death and dying, or who is inclined to think that giving them propositional expression and rational justification is a simple and straightforward matter. Decisions made in the course of the care of the terminally ill are indeed made 'in the smoke-filled room'. However, none of this helps Gillett's case one iota since in so far as it casts doubt on the morality of actively terminating a patient's life in accordance with their wishes, so it also, and to the same extent, casts doubt on the morality of allowing them to die in accordance with their wishes; unless, that is, there is a morally relevant distinction between killing and letting die. But, of course, whether there is such a distinction is precisely the point at issue.

It might be thought that this is to overlook the difference between an active intervention on the one hand and a decision simply to allow nature to take its course on the other. Expressed this way, one might be tempted to think that the moral relevance of the distinction was intuitively obvious. But this would be to ignore the important sense in which we can rightly be held responsible for negative actions, or in other words, intentional acts of forbearance. In one passage Gillett says

> In order to discuss the morality of active euthanasia, we must recall that actions are interventions in the world performed for reasons held by the agent. These reasons usually take account of morally relevant features of situations.[7]

Quite so. But it must also be recalled that negative actions (which by definition are not interventions and yet may or may not involve bodily movement on the part of the clinician) are also performed for reasons held by the agent; reasons which again, in the context of the care of terminally ill patients, usually take account of morally relevant features of situations. It is precisely because the carrying out of a decision not to prevent death is a negative action performed for reasons based on perceived morally relevant features of the situation that doctors are rightly held to be responsible for such actions. Sometimes these negative actions are judged to be morally justified and sometimes not. The point is that any scepticism regarding the moral justification of active euthanasia which is based on doubts concerning the possibility of capturing in propositional form all the subtle moral nuances which pervade the circumstances of the dying patient must equally apply to decisions to allow the patient to die. These also are moral decisions made in 'the smoke-filled room'; unless, of course, it is true that there is a morally relevant distinction between the decision actively to terminate the life of the patient and the decision not to prevent the patient's death. But once again, because this is just the point at issue, to assume it to be true is a flagrant instance of begging the question.

Oddly enough, in one passage Gillett seems to concede the point made in the above paragraph:

> We might . . . ask why the patient requesting [active] euthanasia cannot 'listen to the wisdom of his body' when he formulates his request. If he cannot adequately formulate his reasons, we have argued that he need not. Why, then, do we not allow his request to count as expressing the fact that his life has reached its culmination when he requests [active] euthanasia? *Why do we only accede to the patient's request when it concurs with the entrenched medical opinion which disfavours [active] euthanasia but allows us to let a person die?*[8]

Why indeed? Gillett's answer to his own question essentially consists of a further appeal to intuition which he believes is supported by "a range of subtle differences in the particularities of situations".[9]

At this point it is worth remembering that those who have argued that the killing/letting die distinction is morally irrelevant have not of course denied that there is indeed a real distinction between killing a person and letting them die. What they have argued is that where commonly recognised morally relevant factors, such as motive, presence or absence of consent, expected outcome, are all identical, then actively killing a person and intentionally refraining from preventing their death are morally equivalent in those circumstances.

One way of countering this position would be to concede that the above mentioned morally relevant features are indeed the same but insist that nevertheless there remains a morally relevant difference not philosophically demonstrable but intuitively perceivable by those who have the care of the terminally ill. This seems to be the burden of much of Gillett's article, especially in those passages where he suggests that there is a "holistic particularity to dying situations that does not admit piecemeal reduction to a series of factors, each of which can be shown to be morally irrelevant." The weakness of this intuitive approach should by now be apparent.

Another way of countering the argument would be to insist that, in the context of the care of the dying, the foreseeable outcomes of the pair of cases are not the same, and that it is this difference in likely consequences which constitutes the morally relevant difference. All objections to active euthanasia which allude to a 'slippery slope' are of this form. What is interesting is that, in parts IV and V of his discussion, Gillett seems to abandon the argument 'from moral perception' and instead proceeds to describe a set of concerns relating to the practice of active euthanasia which amount to identifying some of the adverse consequences which that practice would have on society in general and the medical profession in particular.

Two points need to be noticed here. Firstly, arguments directed against the moral acceptability of active euthanasia are not in themselves arguments against the moral irrelevance of the distinction between killing and letting die, since if that distinction is morally irrelevant in the circumstances in which the outcome is the same, such arguments simply amount to objections to passive euthanasia as well. But we have already seen that Gillett is in favour of passive euthanasia in certain circumstances. Hence, to accept passive euthanasia, and argue against active euthanasia does not of itself constitute an argument against the moral irrelevance of the distinction. What is also required is a demonstration that the reasons why passive euthanasia is acceptable do not apply to active euthanasia, and the reasons why active euthanasia is unacceptable do not apply to passive euthanasia. No such demonstration is supplied.

It is true that if the practice of active euthanasia were to have the adverse consequences for society and the medical profession that Gillett and other critics of active euthanasia expect, this would certainly be morally relevant to the question under discussion. However, two important points need to be addressed. Firstly, reasonably good empirical evidence is required to support the view that the alleged adverse consequences would in fact be a probable outcome. It is not impossible that such evidence could be provided, and the best prospects for obtaining it would be from a carefully conducted scientific study of a society which has introduced the practice. Conceivably, the situation in the Netherlands provides such an opportunity and there have been some who have claimed that studies of this country's practice have already confirmed the fears of those who oppose active euthanasia. Others, however, have seen reason to question the methodology of those studies and the interpretation of their conclusions.[10] Arguably, a lot more research of a high quality needs to be done before any firm conclusions can be drawn. What is certain is that anecdotal evidence of the kind that Gillett provides in part IV of his discussion is totally inadequate to support the prediction that the dire social consequences which he describes would follow the introduction of active euthanasia.

Secondly, even if it were clear that allowing the practice of active euthanasia would have adverse social consequences (and, moreover, that it would not be possible to set in place measures that would eliminate or minimise them), this would need to be balanced against the adverse social consequences of the present practice of disallowing that practice. That there are such consequences is certainly not a matter of speculation even if their extent and degree of seriousness is controversial. A judgment as to which of the two scenarios constitutes the greater evil would then be required and might indeed turn out to be a difficult exercise. What seems clear is that evaluating the social consequences of people coming to regard active and passive voluntary euthanasia as being morally equivalent is a complex matter requiring careful examination of relevant evidence obtained by the best available methodologies of the social sciences.

It is ironical that those who have argued for their equivalence have typically done so by employing carefully detailed consequentialist arguments to show that, in situations where the expected outcome is virtually identical, any moral objections against active euthanasia apply equally to passive euthanasia. Of course, these arguments may nevertheless be unsound. The appropriate way to reject their conclusion, therefore, is to show just where they have gone wrong. Unfortunately this is a strategy that Gillett quite deliberately avoids.

It is worth pointing out that what is characteristic of those who have employed consequentialist arguments for the moral irrelevance of the distinction in question is the conviction that the particular circumstances and probable consequences of any individual action are always morally relevant and so must be attended to with some care. It is therefore singularly inappropriate to defend the alleged moral relevance of the distinction by appealing to "a range of subtle differences in the particularities of situations," as if those who reject the moral relevance of the distinction are failing to do this. Precisely the reverse is true. For to deny that the distinction is morally relevant is certainly not to assert that that there is never any morally relevant distinction to be drawn between killing and letting die. This is asserted to be true only in those relatively rare circumstances where the agent has both the ability and opportunity to prevent death and where the outcome of either killing or letting die can reasonably be expected to be the same. Deciding when these conditions occur necessarily involves paying careful attention to 'the particularities of situations'. If therefore any can be accused of failing to do just that, it is surely those who insist that the distinction is always morally relevant. If we know intuitively that it is always worse to kill rather than to let die, and that for the medical practitioner to do the latter is sometimes justifiable but to do the former never, then although taking account of the "particularities of situations" would be relevant to deciding whether it was appropriate to allow the patient to die, it would be quite irrelevant to deciding whether, in the circumstances, this was morally equivalent to killing the patient.

In summary, Gillett is surely right in identifying the moral relevance or irrelevance of the killing/letting die distinction as being of crucial importance to the ethics of euthanasia. Moreover, those whose profession brings them into intimate association with the dying and terminally ill are well placed to draw to the attention of those who lack this opportunity morally relevant facts which those who have denied the moral relevance of the distinction may have overlooked. However, I have argued that the attempt to do this by means of appeals to moral perceptions or intuitions available only to the privileged few is both question-begging and unhelpful. Furthermore, Gillett's reiterated insistence on the importance of attending to the particularities of situations, far from helping his case, has simply helped to highlight its weaknesses. It does not, of course, follow that those who have argued for the opposing point of view are correct. But if they are not, then (pace Gillett) there is no substitute for clear, logically cogent arguments to show this. But, paradoxically, although as a clinician he purports to despise such arguments, he believes that his own discussion nevertheless does constitute an 'argument', and some of it certainly does. I have tried to show that, where argument is indeed present, it is seriously lacking in cogency. If he believes I have succeeded, I suspect that, as a philosopher, he would find this fact disturbing after all.

Notes

1. 'Killing, letting die and moral perception' *Bioethics* 8:4 (1994), pp. 312–328.
2. p. 313 (my emphasis). See also p. 328.
3. p. 328.
4. p. 313.

5. p. 316.
6. p. 315.
7. p. 314.
8. p. 323 (my emphasis).
9. p. 323.
10. For a good discussion of the difficulties in interpreting the evidence trom the practice of active euthanasia in the Netherlands, see Battin, 'A dozen caveats concerning the discussion of euthanasia in the Netherlands', in M.Battin, *The Least Worst Death: essays in bioethics on the end of life* (New York, OUP, 1994), pp.130–144.

13
A Sceptic's Tale

My religious scepticism is a by-product of studying philosophy

Let me say right away that my journey from Christian belief to religious scepticism was principally a by-product of my becoming a professional philosopher, even though the transition took a period of some years. I'm aware that some believers might argue that such a change was only to be expected and see it as evidence of the dangers of studying philosophy. Modern western science and philosophy, a product of the 18th century enlightenment, is often seen as characterised by an arrogant faith in human reason, and therefore as necessarily the enemy of religious faith. No wonder that those who study it are more than likely to find themselves bereft of spiritual values and deprived of any capacity for discerning life's true meaning. So it might be argued.

Putting aside for the moment the fact that some of the greatest thinkers in the western philosophical tradition have been the most sceptical concerning the scope and power of human reason, I shall argue that, at least in my own case, the transition to religious unbelief as a consequence of my study of philosophy has been a positive, enriching and liberating experience. I shall contend that respect for human reason is the opposite of arrogance, and that the philosophical tradition in which I stand has contributed enormously to our understanding of questions concerning the nature of values and life's meaning, thus providing us with a better foundation for distinguishing intelligible from confused forms of these questions, and hence for recognising plausible as opposed to spurious answers to them.

My religious upbringing

My religous upbringing was in conventional, middle-church Anglicanism. By the time I was in my late teens I was a member of the parish church choir, involved in youth group activities at both the parish and diocesan level, and inspired with the idealism typical of many young men of the immediate post-war era. As a regular church attender and member of a Bible class, I absorbed the kind of instruction in the Anglican tradition of the Christian faith that must have been delivered to many of my contemporaries. Though I was never a 'fundamentalist', at 18 or thereabouts I was convinced that Christianity was fundamentally true, and that it therefore had nothing to fear from critical enquiry. Moreover, I believed the Gospel message of the victorious power of the love of God to be of such great importance that I wanted to devote my life in trying to persuade others to share this faith, and to live by it. Consequently, I offered myself for ordination. After acquiring an arts degree in philosophy, and some moderate qualifications in theology, at the age of 27 I was duly ordained priest, and served my curacy in Wellington's beautiful old Cathedral Church of St Paul.

Academic ambitions

By this stage I had become aware that my principal interests in Christianity were academic and I had already begun to entertain hopes that eventually I might obtain a position as a lecturer in a theological college. These hopes were realised sooner than I had anticipated. After only a brief period as a vicar in the remote country parish of Mangaweka, I was offered, and accepted, the post of chaplain-tutor at College House in Christchurch, which at that time was still functioning as a theological college. I was given the responsibility of teaching Christian doctrine. However, because of my background in philosophy, it was the philosophy of religion that was of particular interest to me. In the philosophical world in the 1950s and 1960s, at least in

Anglo-American and Commonwealth universities, this subject was undergoing something of a revival, having suffered years of comparative neglect. The heyday of the analytic movement was at its height and philosophers who were interested in religion were discovering that the analytical techniques of twentieth century thinkers (like Wittgenstein, Ryle, and Austin) were providing a new approach to some old problems.

When in 1961 Religious Studies was introduced at Canterbury University it was my interest in the philosophy of religion that led to my being appointed to the Philosophy Department to teach that subject as part of the Religious Studies programme. I was still an officiating minister in the Anglican Church, but because of my involvement in teaching the philosophy of religion I found myself more than ever before having to face up to the intellectual difficulties which confront anyone who is both a philosopher and a committed Christian.

Tension between the search for truth and Christian commitment

In particular, it was the ideal of Christian commitment that began to trouble me. I had always taken it for granted that a genuine Christian was a committed Christian, but I began to ask myself what "commitment" means, and how it differs from a determination to hold fast to something no matter what happens. If the 'something' is a belief, or set of beliefs, and if 'what happens' is the turning up of evidence that weighs against those beliefs, it seemed to me that such commitment looked uncomfortably like wilful prejudice. How could a genuine student or scholar properly acknowledge any other commitment than to the search for the truth? Nor was the difficulty removed if it was pointed out that Christian commitment is to Jesus Christ rather than to a set of beliefs. It is scarcely possible, or even intelligible, to commit oneself to Jesus without holding some minimal core of historical beliefs about him, and this minimal core would have to involve more than the well-attested belief that he was indeed an historical figure who was "crucified under Pontius Pilate." The further historical beliefs which would be relevant to any religious commitment are precisely those whose supporting evidence is dubious and controversial, or at best less than conclusive. From the point of view of academic integrity, this would surely call for no more than provisional acceptance, if not suspense of judgment.

The problem which history raises for orthodox Christian belief

I struggled with this conflict between Christian commitment and intellectual integrity for some years and became increasingly dissatisfied with the attempts of Christian scholars to resolve it. Christian historians like Herbert Butterfield seemed to me to fail to understand just how serious the difficulties are if one accepts the traditional view that, in a special sense, Christianity is a 'historical' religion. I take that special sense to be that the truth of certain historical claims about Jesus of Nazareth is a necessary, though not sufficient, condition for the truth of its central religious doctrines. Christian philosophers like Basil Mitchell, who at least understood the problem, failed to satisfy me that they had solved it. Just how serious the problem is for the traditional interpretation of Christianity was forcibly drawn to my attention by R. W. Hepburn's book *Christianity and Paradox*. His two chapters entitled 'Historicity and Risk' should be compulsory reading for any Christian who has not realised that what used at one time to be thought of as a unique and superior feature of the Christian religion, viz. that it is rooted and grounded in the facts of history, is the very feature which inevitably drives a wedge between Christian commitment and intellectual integrity. As an academic discipline, history in its very nature is subject to the possibility of revision in the light of emerging new evidence. No responsible historian, therefore, can be committed to the truth of any claim about what has happened in the past, let alone claims about the remote past. Moreover if those claims include an assertion to the effect that Jesus rose from the dead on the third day after his crucifixion, and if the only historical evidence for this claim is to be found in certain documents, written by Jesus' followers who apparently worshipped him as God, then any modern historians who declared that they were committed to the truth of this assertion would surely reveal themselves to be unworthy to be regarded as responsible historians. Or so it seemed to me. Yet the traditional Christian view, whether it be Catholic, Protestant or Eastern Orthodox, is that unless the resurrection is indeed a historical fact, the central doctrines of the Christian religion are false. How then could any honest person who understands what it means to be a responsible historian be a committed Christian?

A possible solution to the problem

Of course one way to avoid the dilemma is simply to deny that the essential truths of Christianity are bound up with the historicity of certain events which took place in the remote past. In recent years this has been the route followed by a number of theologians, and for a while I was attracted to it myself. If the historical claims in the NT are irrelevant to the spiritual and moral insights that it contains, then one can certainly profit from those insights, whether or not the stories in which they are embedded are factually true. Furthermore, it is at least questionable whether the Gospels were ever in fact *intended* to be interpreted as including historical assertions whose factual truth is an essential component of their spiritual message. But when theologians like Bishop John Robinson popularised the severance of the spiritual message of Christianity from its traditional historical foundations, he was widely criticised by both believers and unbelievers alike as having so distorted and emasculated the essence of the Christian Gospel as to have made it unrecognisably Christian. The baby had been thrown out with the bathwater.

But what is the 'essence' of Christianity?

It is difficult to avoid begging questions as soon as one alludes to the 'essence' of Christianity, since it is far from clear what should be the appropriate criteria by which one distinguishes those doctrines or ideas which constitute the essential core of the Christian religion from those which can be regarded as peripheral and dispensable accretions which (to change the metaphor) comprise no more than the cultural packaging determined by its provenance. As one wit had put it, one man's baby is apt to be another man's bathwater. In short, it seemed to me that both the conservative Christians and the bemused atheists had too simplistic an understanding of what is involved in either accepting or rejecting the central doctrines of Christianity, since it is so difficult to reach any agreement concerning what is to count as 'central'.

Not only does this apply to the question of how much (if any) historical truth in the Gospel records is essential to Christianity but it is also relevant to the question whether belief in God is itself a necessary ingredient of that religion. Of course even now it is rare for bishops and theologians to deny outright that they believe in God. But it is increasingly common for theism to be so loosely interpreted that, when spelt out in plain language, it appears to the ordinary layperson to be indistinguishable from atheism.

Do labels matter?

Perhaps not. What you call a system of religious belief is a relatively trivial point. What matters is whether that system of belief expresses the truth. For a while I was attracted to this point of view. I saw what I took to be the central message of Christianity as essentially expressing values which should determine the shape and direction of a Christian's life. The linguistic and culturally determined medium which conveys and gives meaning and power to these values I took to be no more than the medium, and not part of the message itself. From this point of view, to believe that God is love (for example) is not necessarily to believe that there exists some supernatural personal or quasi-personal spiritual being whose essential nature is to love. Rather, it is to declare that love is the supreme value, and that, in the end, love will triumph over all evils.Whether so interpreted this is still Christianity seemed unimportant. When, at this period of my life, people asked me if I regarded myself as a Christian, I would reply, "I'll tell you what I believe – you tell me if I am a Christian." I suspect that this point of view, or something very like it, is shared by a great many thinking and liberal-minded people of today who are fairly regular church attenders, and who systematically, as it were, reinterpret all that is said or sung in church more or less along the lines I have just described.

Tension between private belief and public worship

At this stage of my spiritual pilgrimage I was still an ordained priest of the Anglican Church. Although as a university lecturer I had no regular ecclesiastical responsibilities, from time to time I would be asked to take a service for a parish vicar who was sick or on holiday. As one who was required to lead worship, even if only occasionally, I became increasingly aware of the huge gap between what I believed to be the important substance of religious language and what the ordinary person in the pew was quite reasonably taking to be the plain meaning of the words that were being said and sung in church. Moreover, if the essential meaning of religious language is what I took it to be, it was surely highly misleading to convey that message in language that inevitably suggests something quite different; namely, that there really is an infinitely good, wise and powerful, spiritual Being who exists independently of us and the world; a Being who loves us, and with whom we can be in some kind of personal relationship, and who hears our prayers and hymns of praise. Since I no longer believed that any of this is true, it seemed irresponsible to occupy a role which inevitably suggested that I did. So, in 1967 I went to Bishop Pyatt and relinquished my licence as an officiating minister. (I still think that the most useful and direct way of discovering just what a person's religious belief [or unbelief] amounts to is to ask them just what they think is going on when people engage in prayer and worship.)

The misleading nature of God-talk cleansed of belief in the supernatural

I now believe that reinterpreting Christian religious belief in terms of values which have been 'cleansed' of all traces of the supernatural is a mistake. It unquestionably has an attraction for those who have been brought up in the context of the Christian tradition and who wish to do justice to the moral insights which that tradition has provided, but who are also deeply conscious of the intellectual difficulties surrounding traditional Christian theology. Nevertheless, it has rightly been observed that if God language is simply a picturesque way of talking about values and human relationships, then this can be done much more clearly, and far less misleadingly, simply by talking about values and human relationships. Of course, to persist in indulging in God-talk does have a certain attraction for 'nouveau' atheists who have a nostalgia for the colour and symbolism of religious language.

The value and shortcomings of poetry and myth

Admittedly, it would be a mistake to overlook the importance of poetry and myth in providing a dynamic and motivating power lacking in typically abstract philosophical talk about values. There is no doubt that parables and mythical stories can be extremely effective in stimulating the moral imagination. It would be sheer folly to neglect them just because they originated in a cultural context in which belief in the supernatural was as much an integral part of the intellectual world of the time as the scientific attitude is of our own. Nevertheless, popular talk about poetry and myth as constituting a rich source of 'spiritual truths' often overlooks the fact that poetry and myth can also be rich sources of 'spiritual falsehoods'. For example, there can be little doubt that the mythology contained in a vast amount of sacred literature, the Bible not excluded, often portrays women as having a divinely ordained inferior status. Once it is recognised that myths can convey falsehoods as well as truths, it becomes clearer that the only way of determining the truth-value of what is being conveyed by any particular myth is to subject it to some kind of rational, critical analysis.

Faith and reason

So far I have said nothing about faith. It might be objected that my background of Western philosophy has blinded me to the crucial role of faith in Christian religious belief, and provided me with a naïve if not arrogant belief in the power of human reason, a belief which is seen as much an act of faith as any religious commitment. If no one, whether religious believer or unbeliever, can avoid making an act of faith, can there really be any valid intellectual objection to religious faith? This question is important and certainly deserves to be addressed. To deal with it adequately would require a lengthy discussion, but I will comment briefly on what I take to be the main issues.

The need to recognise the fallibility of reason

It is far from easy to say what exactly it means to talk about 'human reason' but whatever it is, it is certainly a fallible capacity. We may not be the only animals on this planet that can be properly said to think, but we are probably the only species that has the capacity to reflect critically on our thinking.

Critical reflection involves reasoning, which basically consists of asserting (or denying) things on the basis of other things that have been asserted or denied. We have developed criteria for distinguishing good reasoning from bad. (This is the business of logic.) Good reasoning is the sort that preserves us from straying from the truth, provided that the starting point of our reasoning (our premisses) is not in error. But no matter how careful we are in our reasoning, in actual practice it is always possible for us to go wrong. Fallibility is part of the human condition. I cannot see any justification for calling this understanding of human reason "faith."

The ambiguity of 'faith'

'Faith' as the term is used in the context of religious belief is apt to be a rather slippery concept. Its most respectable meaning is when it is used to convey something akin to trust. If the object of religious belief is a God who has at least some of the characteristics of personhood (including a capacity to give and receive love), then having faith is certainly an integral part of the Christian religious attitude, since any kind of personal or quasi-personal relationship worthy of the name involves trust. To have faith in God, then, is to have trust in God. But it is important to notice that, in this sense, having faith in God presupposes that God exists. Belief in God's existence cannot itself be a matter of faith in this sense, unless it is faith in something or someone other than God. Put in its most general form, this means that if one has faith in x (whatever x may be) then belief in the existence of x must be on the basis of something other than faith in x. It cannot make sense to trust God not to let us down by not existing.

A less respectable interpretation of the meaning of the word "faith" is when the concept is used to convey the notion of absence of good reasons, or worse, of opposition to good reasons. When a person claims that their religious belief is founded on faith, do they want to be understood as saying that they haven't the slightest reason for thinking that their belief is true? Surely not. I suspect that usually they are either guilty of the muddle I've just described, or else they want to make the point that they are not in a position to prove that their belief is true. Fair enough. But they do think that their belief is well-founded, because it is based on their own personal experience. My guess is that the vast majority of thoughtful religious believers who appeal to faith as the basis of their belief are implicitly alluding to their own personal religious or spiritual experience as providing that basis. Appeals to religious experience are typically regarded as being immune to rational criticism because of their private and personal nature. They are seen as bypassing any kind of rational argument and as providing an immediate, intuitive, self-authenticating and therefore secure foundation for religious belief. Something like this was once my own conviction.

Religious experience is always an interpreted experience

The fundamental weakness of appeals to religious experience as a basis for belief is the mistaken assumption that they constitute a genuine alternative to an appeal to reason. Certainly, the owners of an experience are the authorities on whether they have had an experience of some sort or other; but almost any kind of experience is an interpreted experience, which is capable of being misinterpreted by the subject who has it. This is certainly true of religious or spiritual experiences.To deny that an experience is self-authenticating is not of course to deny that the believer has had an experience of some sort; it is simply to draw attention to the fact that the owner of the experience could be misreading its meaning. In other words, they may be taking it to have implications and a significance which it does not in fact possess. Experiences of any sort virtually never come to us uninterpreted. They are always in an important sense 'theory-laden,' even though the 'theory' has not been consciously or explicitly entertained, but rather acquired through a combination of cultural and physiological factors which determine and shape our perception of the world. This point even applies to such immediate and simple examples as the experience of pain. When someone claims to have a pain, it is hard to see how they could be mistaken. Yet, if they claim, quite sincerely, to have a pain in their right foot, they conceivably could be mistaken. Their very report of their experience encapsulates an interpretation which could be mistaken. This is actually the case with amputees who experience phantom pains. A person cannot have a pain in a foot which does not exist.

Now whereas claims like "I have a pain in my right foot" involve a minimum of 'theory' (and therefore a relatively small potential for mistake), religious claims made on the basis of experience tend to encapsulate a great deal of interpretation (or 'theory'), with a correspondingly large potential for error. If therefore appeals to faith are covert appeals to personal experience as a basis for belief, then it is certainly not true that such appeals constitute an alternative to appeals to reason, since the question will always arise whether one is misinterpreting one's experience. Facing up to this question inescapably involves having to make use of one's capacity for rational, critical reflection.

In short, if 'faith' means trust, then it is not, and cannot be, an alternative to reason, since one cannot have faith or trust in a being or reality that one literally has no reason whatever to believe exists. And if one's own personal experience is viewed as providing that reason, the honest reflective person cannot avoid considering the possibility that they may be misinterpreting that experience, a consideration that necessarily involves the use of the human ability to reason. None of these reflections seems to me to imply human arrogance or overweening hubris, since the human capacity for critical reasoning is neither unlimited nor infallible. The point is simply that we cannot avoid the use of our reason if we are to reflect on these matters at all. Indeed, recognising both the inescapable as well as the fallible features of this capacity is surely the very antithesis of arrogance.

Are we responsible for what we believe, or disbelieve?

In the Judeo-Christian as well as the Islamic tradition, apostasy has typically been regarded as a great sin, but it has not always been noticed that there is an important respect in which what we believe is not in any direct sense a matter of the will, and therefore apparently not something for which we could intelligibly be held responsible. We cannot simply decide to believe, or disbelieve. This is because believing is not a kind of mental act or activity, but rather something like a mental state or disposition. An atheist can no more 'decide to believe' any more than believers are capable of deciding to give up their belief. This is not because of human limitations but simply a matter of the logic of belief. Nevertheless, there is a sense in which we can and ought to take responsibility for our beliefs. Although believing or disbelieving something to be true is not an act or activity, there are things that we can do which will have an effect on what it is that we believe or disbelieve. For example, we can attend to, or refuse to attend to, what could be relevant evidence for the truth of our beliefs. The former is what a judge exhorts the members of a jury to do when they are asked to make up their minds (decide) whether the accused is guilty or innocent. In effect, they are exhorted to allow the evidence, and only the evidence, to determine their belief.

It is certainly true that what we believe on any matter can be, and often is, determined by a large range of causal factors which have nothing to do with the truth or falsity of our beliefs. Such factors are prejudice, wishful thinking, propaganda, high pressure advertising, emotional rhetoric, brainwashing, drugs, etc. Factors like these can be enormously effective determinants of what we believe, even though these causes are quite independent of the facts which determine whether our beliefs are true or false. Taking responsibility for our beliefs then involves trying to bring it about that the causes of our beliefs are not divorced from what would be relevant to their truth. This amounts to a resolution to seek out and respect relevant evidence, to listen and attend to rational objections to our beliefs, and to try to allow ourselves to be guided by sound argument, wherever it may lead. Of course, being human we will not always succeed, for pride, prejudice, pigheadedness, and plain stupidity will often get in the way. But the goal remains clear. Because we are human, the truth will often elude us, but if we are serious about seeking after it, I believe there is no likelihood of finding it in any other way.

The ethics of belief

Just what we believe certainly matters a great deal, and in the context of religious belief, the facile aphorism 'It doesn't matter what you believe, so long as you are sincere' deserves a firm rejection. It would be better to say that it doesn't matter what you believe so long as you are insincere. Insincere beliefs have little or no effect on our actions and are likely to be relatively harmless. On the other hand, sincere religious beliefs, can have, and have had, important consequences – consequences both for human misery as well as human happiness which are literally incalculable. As the 18th century philosopher David Hume once remarked, "Generally speaking, errors in religion are dangerous. Errors in philosophy are only ridiculous." Thus there is such a thing as the ethics of belief, even though belief is not directly a matter of the will. Once it is understood how it is that what we believe can indirectly be within our control, the obligation to do what we can to ensure that our beliefs are determined by nothing other than what is relevant to their truth is one which no thoughtful person would want to shirk.

The unpopularity of taking rationality seriously

Nevertheless, it has to be conceded that taking rationality seriously has little appeal for many people. Some fear it because of the uncertainty of its outcome. To follow the argument wherever it leads is not to know in advance where it will lead. Not a few nineteenth century Christian scholars, who faithfully adhered to this Socratic advice, found the consequent loss of their Christian faith deeply disturbing, and one from which they never fully recovered. My own experience has been quite different. The sense of exhilaration and excitement that is involved in welcoming rational enquiry into one's fundamental beliefs is something that I have relished. Far from producing a feeling of insecurity, for me it has had the opposite effect. If you prefer your beliefs to be true, then you are always immune from the damaging effects of any soundly based attack on your beliefs, since once you are convinced of the soundness of an opposing viewpoint, it then becomes your own. Consequently, you have the enviable advantage of always occupying the higher ground. Of course this does not mean that you have arrived at the truth, but it does mean that your beliefs have the best support available to you at the time. It is part of our human condition that there is no 'hot line' to the truth.

The debit and credit aspects of religious scepticism

It must be acknowledged that becoming convinced that there is no good reason to believe that there is a God involves a realisation that certain other beliefs which one would prefer to be true are regrettably without good foundation. I once was convinced that a God of love who was also the creator of the universe would, as it were, see to it that ultimately love would triumph over all evils, including the pain of being permanently separated by death from loved ones. I now view the belief that good will eventually triumph over evil as naïve rather than baseless. 'Good' and 'evil' are not spiritual forces but abstract concepts derived from our value judgments, which are themselves grounded in our fundamental goals and preferences. Recognising that our moral convictions have a human rather than a divine foundation renders them no less important and a great deal more intelligible. Indeed, a study of the history of the belief that the distinction between right and wrong is founded on the authority of God's will reveals that, with a few exceptions, even Christian theologians rejected this theory as being itself morally repugnant, since it implies that moral distinctions are ultimately arbitrary. Our conviction that grossly immoral acts such as torture and rape are indeed immoral does not lie easily with a belief that they would be morally acceptable if God had not forbidden them. Of course, a wholly good God necessarily would forbid them, but then the conviction that God is wholly good cannot itself, without circularity, be based on God's will, but must rest on a human moral judgment. Coming to see the sense in which moral judgments are inescapably autonomous and cannot without incoherence be based on any moral authority, whether divine or human, can be an important step in arriving at a clearer understanding of the nature of morality. As to life after death, I am now persuaded that the available evidence to date overwhelmingly points to the conclusion that human beings, like all other animals on this planet, are destined to inevitable mortality. Moreover, issues relating to the concept of personal identity make it doubtful that the idea of personal survival of bodily death is even logically coherent, in which case not even the existence of an omnipotent deity could make it true that after we die we will be reunited with those whom we love. This conviction does nothing to lessen the pain of separation which is indeed terribly real. But if it deprives us of the hope of being reunited with our loved ones, it also dispels fears and worries about 'the great unknown', fears and worries which over the centuries have been only too real for countless millions of people. Death's sting is indeed real for the bereaved living; but with regard to one's own death, it makes no more sense to be concerned about nonexistence after death than about nonexistence before conception (as Epicurus pointed out in the 4th century B.C.)

Epilogue

It seems appropriate to conclude this tale with a tribute to David Hume, the 18th century Scottish philosopher who, more than any other has influenced my attitude towards both religion and life itself. For me, Hume has the distinction of drawing attention to the limits of human reason and at the same time, in his discussion of religious belief, deploying his own possession of this faculty with consummate skill and devastating effectiveness. His *Dialogues Concerning Natural Religion*, arguably the most important contribution to the philosophy of religion in the English language, provides an exemplary model of how religious belief can be intelligently and critically discussed. Although a relatively short book compared with his massive *Treatise on Human Nature*, Hume spent more time in writing and constantly revising the *Dialogues* than any of his other philosophical works – which is some indication of the measure of importance he attached to the philosophical examination of religious belief. But perhaps above all I admire Hume for his enviable success in harmonising his philosophical reflections with his personal life. In an age when scepticism concerning the existence of God and life after death was far from being regarded as respectable, even in academic circles,

Hume's personal life was such that even those who wanted to hate him often found that, on personal acquaintance, his kind, genial and good-humoured nature completely won them over. To my knowledge, no other philosopher has been more diligent in fearlessly following the argument wherever it leads, and none more successful in maintaining a sane, balanced and cheerful outlook on practical life. Socrates has been rightly revered for the manner in which he met his death. But unlike Socrates, whose serenity was due in large measure to his conviction that he was about to enter upon another and more worthwhile existence, when Hume was dying of cancer he had no such reassuring hope. Even when questioned at this stage by the curious and insensitive Boswell who had hoped to witness a death-bed repentance, Hume's calm, witty and clearheaded rejection of any expectation of a future life impressed even Boswell himself. In short, Hume in his own life demonstrated to all students of philosophy both the wisdom as well as the achievable nature of his advice: "Be a philosopher, but amidst all your philosophy, be still a man."

References

R. W. Hepburn, *Christianity and Paradox* (London, Watts, 1958).

David Hume, *Dialogues Concerning Natural Religion* (1779).

Postscript

This essay is a slightly modified version of an article which was first published as a contribution to *Journeymen: Essays on Male Spirituality*, edited by Robin Barrett and John Fisher (Publishing Giant Press, Christchurch, 1999). Unlike most of the other papers in this collection, this essay was never intended to be read by professional philosophers but was simply addressed to the general reading public. However, by chance it came into the hands of my former Professor, Bob Stoothoff, who thought it certainly deserved to be published more widely. He passed it on to Professor Jack Smart, formerly of the Research School of A.N.U. at Canberra, and also to Ray Bradley, formerly Professor of Philosophy at the University of Auckland. Both praised it enthusiastically. Hence its inclusion in this collection.

www.ingramcontent.com/pod-product-compliance
Ingram Content Group UK Ltd.
Pitfield, Milton Keynes, MK11 3LW, UK
UKHW041855190726
13854UKWH00002B/919